Steve's personal catharsi:
past disappointments, sir
Adam and have his fallei
sin. In this book, people c
through Jesus Christ.

—Jim Richards, Executive Director
Southern Baptists of Texas Convention

With wit, insight, and painful transparency Steve Hunter shows us in a biblical manner how to have true joy in the locker room of life—freeing ourselves from sin, the need to prove ourselves or compare with others. If you don't struggle in these areas, this book will help you minister to others that do. Steve's greatest desire is to glorify Christ and to help others walk with the Lord. This book does that!

—Rodney L. Hammer, Regional Leader
Central and Eastern Europe, International Mission Board
Southern Baptist Convention

Steve Hunter forces us to examine the authenticity of our walk with the Lord and the faith we confess. With brutal honesty the author reflects on his own bondage to following the forms of traditional religion and church life while denying the sham, shame, and hypocrisy of ungodly attitudes and self-centered motivation. The book is painful and convicting to read but well worth getting to the final chapter and discovering practical steps to experiencing the liberating grace of God and being set free to a victorious walk in Christ.

—Jerry Rankin, President
International Mission Board, SBC

Make-Believers is a spirit-filled account that takes you into the heart of worship as you explore the reality of the person God has created each of us to be and the identity of the believer in Jesus Christ. Dr. Steve Hunter shares a personal account from the heart. Using the analogy of a theatrical performance he uses his own life experiences to help present an amazing picture of the reality of the different experiences that each believer goes through. This is a must-read for any believer who is ready to relinquish control and allow God to assume authority in his or her life and for those who are ready to learn more about their identity in Christ.

—Dr. Nicole Fitzpatrick, Psychologist
Hyde Park Baptist Counseling Center, Austin

Hooray for Dr. Hunter in speaking so transparently about something so many of us can relate to at some point in our lives in "playing at Christianity." *Make-Believers* exposes shame for what it is—a painful emotion which leads to a life based on false beliefs and false deception. Read the book and find hope and the secret to a truly transformed life!

—Pam Green, Director
Pathways Center for Christian Counseling, Dallas

I have read many "counseling books" but none such as this one. It is a transparent, intimate, and God-ordained book. I was touched, encouraged, inspired, and made to cry by what Dr. Hunter presented so graphically. It will be a highly valuable resource in the hands of competent counselors for many years from now, I'm sure. Many small groups will find it a powerful tool in gaining freedom from "Make-Believing."

—Wallace B. Cobb, Retired Director of Pastoral Ministries
Champion Forest Baptist Church, Houston, TX

This book is dangerous! It will bring you to grips with the subconscious superficiality that lurks within us all. May God use this book to set many "make-believers" free.

—Scott Camp, International Evangelist and Pastor
Fellowship of Joy Church, Mansfield, TX

Wonderfully written! With an understanding through life experiences, Dr. Hunter is able to identify reasoning and pitfalls in a performance-driven life. Having experienced his own healing from God's grace, he walks readers through the process of healing and helps them to experience freedom that is found in walking in truth and releasing them to live an abundant life that honors God.

—Alan Lynch, Associate Pastor of Spiritual Development
First Baptist Church, Dallas

Dr. Hunter's heartfelt book is bound to resonate with Christians and with those who merely believe they are Christians. Both his wit and humor serve to lighten this most serious topic of what is meant by living out one's faith on the difficult journey to become who God intends us to be. It is at once sensitive, compelling, and heart-wrenching, but best of all, it demonstrates wisdom through a practical guide that lets his fellow sojourners feel less alone, discover hope, and grow closer to their Lord by faith that yields results.

—Mike Troutt, Louise Herrington School of Nursing
Baylor University, Dallas

Steve Hunter is one of the top professors at Criswell College. This book reveals why Dr. Hunter is the real deal and why he is passionate about helping you realize authentic living in your Christian journey. In *Make-Believers* the combination of Dr. Hunter's life story and biblical truth make for a powerful message. Buy it, read it, give it to a friend.

—Jerry Johnson, President
The Criswell College
Professor of Theology and Ethics

I love this writer! He definitely is honest and a deep thinker. Read his book and experience a more intimate relationship with Christ. By the way, he's also a great husband and dad.

—Karen Hunter, homemaker and mother of six

Make-Believers

Ending the Pretending to Live Happily Ever After

Dr. Steve T. Hunter

Hannibal Books
www.hannibalbooks.com

Printed in the United States of America
by Versa Press, East Peoria, IL
Cover design by Greg Crull
Except where otherwise indicated, Scripture taken
from the Holy Bible, *New International Version*, copyright 1973,
1978, 1984 by International Bible Society
Library of Congress Control Number: 2005934354
ISBN 0-929292-36-7

Hannibal Books
P.O. Box 461592
Garland, TX 75046
1-800-747-0738
www.hannibalbooks.com

Dedication

This book is dedicated to my wife, Karen,
for her undying love.

(Most of the time) She loves me, warts and all.

Foreword

On a recent trip to Malawi, Africa, I gained a new perspective of "the tip of the iceberg." I was teaching *Lead Like Jesus* to missionary leaders on a game reserve situated on the Shire River, which is populated with more than 500 hippopotami. We were warned not to get out at night without a flashlight, because the hippos would wander among our semi-permanent tent houses and attack anything they heard. More people are killed by hippos in Africa than are killed by any other animal, including lions, elephants, and Cape buffalo. I stayed in bed and kept quiet when the hippos moved ashore.

As we cruised the river each morning on a game ride, we could see "pods" of hippos with just their ears and eyes sticking out of the water. Africans have a saying, "That's just the ears of the hippo." Many of our problems appear as "the ears of the hippo", but just beneath the surface lurks the crushing weight of a killer. This book addresses the problems that few of us admit lie submerged just below our consciousness.

You will not be able to put down this book unless it so vividly exposes your problems that you won't read on to face them and to discover the solutions it offers. Steve Hunter, as few counselors have, has opened up his life for us to what makes him tick. He has done it to help us admit our life struggles and to find adequate answers to them. This book has impacted my life and helped me understand myself and others better.

When I first met Steve, I never would have suspected what lurked beneath the surface. For years I had known his wife and in-laws. He was a muscular, good-looking, blond "hunk" and had all the credentials to counsel and to teach. When he became a missionary, he had become so proficient, I could not have guessed what he had experienced or how he had tried to cover up the shame with a *virtuoso* religious performance. Each time I saw him in Central and Eastern Europe and on Stateside assignment, I continued to be impressed. Only when I read the manuscript for this book did I realize what he had undergone and his struggles to cope. As God often does through cross-cultural experiences, He used Steve's experience on the mission field to expose the chinks in the armor. Now, I'm not just impressed with Steve but honored and privileged to know the real believer—the real Christian man he has become.

In this book Steve deals with the issues other counselors address, but he does this by sharing personal, hurtful experiences and helpful, Christian answers. He unmasks several actors who dominate the stages of our lives, but he does it in such an open, unassuming, even humorous, way that you can surface similar feelings in your own buried past. Look for biblical solutions to deal with how you feel.

I heartily recommend that you read all of this book. Some of the most captivating parts of Steve's testimony occur near the end. You will discover how shame, blame, guilt, resentment, and hate torpedo one's life. You find solidly biblical solutions on a deep, spiritual level to enable you to deal with any problems that surface.

Steve Hunter gets to the heart of the matter and shows how you can live an abundant life in Christ by exposing your secret sins and receiving God's full forgiveness and His grace.

Avery T. Willis, Jr.
Emeritus Senior Vice-President of Overseas Operations
International Mission Board of the Southern Baptist Convention

Contents

Preface

If Augustine had been a psychologist/counselor living in the 20th and 21st centuries instead of in the 4th and 5th, his *Confessions* may have sounded like Steve Hunter's *Make-Believers*. In reading both, one clearly sees that the agony of confession and the documentation of a journey lead to freedom, release, and a God-given change. Anyone who suffered at the hands of a bully in early adolescence will weep when reading Dr. Hunter's suffering as a junior-high student. Anyone who, as an adult, struggles with low self-esteem because of childhood experiences will be encouraged by Dr. Hunter's breakthrough.

From a Christian perspective the book charts a journey from defeat to victory, from low self-esteem to high Christ-esteem, from defeat in the flesh to victory in the Spirit, and from struggle to surrender. Theologically Hunter has carefully integrated biblical truth and practical experience. Practically he has constructed a ladder in the shape of the cross on which one can climb out of despair into hope, out of self into Christ, out of a defeated life into a victorious one. The book not only is confessional, it also is instructional. It is about how to move from performance to an authentic Christian life.

Hunter's tremendous ability to mix humor with prayer makes the book highly readable. If a mixture of humor, tears, and spiritual warmth is sound both biblically and psychologically, then this is a very sound book. If the world is looking for authentic Christian living, it will find it in this book written by one who admits his weaknesses, deals with his past, and on his knees climbs bravely into the future, as he embraces the discovery and realization of what being Spirit-filled means. The psychologist, the pastor, and the effective communicator join together in Dr. Hunter's book.

Jim Bryant, Founding Dean of The Criswell College
and Senior Professor of Pastoral Theology

Chapter 1

Setting the Stage

The Lord does not look at the things man looks at. Man looks at the outward appearance, but the Lord looks at the heart (1 Sam. 16:7).

What was your first thought when you saw the title, *Make-Believers*? I bet you thought this was another book on evangelism. By now, you already have figured out that *Make-Believers* is all about Christians who pretend. I hear you asking, "What do you mean by Christians who pretend?" Great question. I believe Christians who pretend have a heart for God but at the same time desire the best the world has to offer. This dualistic pursuit always leads to a dualistic life. Ultimately the things of God provide an "image of goodness" that hides secret sins, secret desires, and secret ambitions. Whenever secrets exists, so does pretending.

My kids love to play and pretend. They enjoy playing different roles and different parts. They always are excited to put on "the big show." The more attention and applause they receive, the better they like it. Often they fuss and fight over who will be the star. I call it "Star Wars." Tragically the same can be true in the Christian life. In their futile attempt to earn love, approval, acceptance, and applause "Make-Believers" pretend or put on a religious show for all to see. The tragedy is that enough applause, enough success, and enough religious accomplishments never are enough to satisfy their deepest, innermost needs.

For the first 20 years of my Christian life I was involved in putting on a show for all to see. In public I was the devoted, dedicated, sacrificial, kind, loving, and forgiving Christian. In private I was controlling, bitter, resentful, discouraged, exhausted, prideful, and completely miserable. I was a Christian, but deep in my heart I felt inadequate, unworthy, unforgivable, and totally unacceptable. How can this be? Was I really saved? Can a Christian genuinely be saved and not be genuine? Why all the pretending, performing, and hiding? Throughout the course of my life these questions have fascinated me and plagued me. These questions are the focus and heart of this book.

Another purpose for writing this book was that during a period of time, I noticed that I was not alone in my struggle. As a counselor, pastor, and professor, I cannot tell you how many times I have heard the statement, "If others knew who I really was, they wouldn't love or even like me." I personally believe that countless Christians hide deep feelings of insecurity and fear while they outwardly strive to prove to God, prove to others, and ultimately prove to themselves they are worthy of love. But why? How do we, as Christians, become trapped in a life of pretending and performing? What does Jesus say about this kind of life? How does a Christian break free to experience a more authentic Christian life? Can the pretending really end? Hang with me; walk with me. You'll see that throughout this book, we will address these very questions. So, the curtain is raised and the show begins . . ..

Lost

I like the television show, *Lost*. It is about a group of people who survived a plane crash and now are stranded and striving to survive on an uncharted island. Each week focuses on one of the characters on the island. At the same time, each week reveals more and more about each character. All of the characters have their secrets. Even the island has its secrets. My favorite part of the show occurs as these secrets slowly are unveiled. For some reason I really like the part when secrets are brought into the light. What we hide makes us unhealthy; our secrets make us sick. Whenever hiding and secrets occur, we also find pretending.

This journey—this book—actually began with a "lost" journal. My family and I served for a little more than seven years as missionaries in Central and Eastern Europe. During that time we moved 14 times. In our move from Kishinev, Moldova, to Prague, Czech Republic, I lost my journal containing my most private, innermost, intimate thoughts and feelings. Not good. After serving as professor of pastoral ministries at The Kishinev College of Theology and Education in the former Soviet Union republic of Moldova, I was invited to be the regional member-care consultant for missionaries serving in 25 countries across 12 time zones throughout Europe. I loved living in Prague. I loved my new position. It fit me like a glove.

One day, out of the clear, blue sky, I received an email from missionary Brad Pollard. Brad and his family moved into the house we occupied in Moldova and continued our ministry there. In his email, Brad wrote, "Steve, I found your journal. It has some good stuff in it. I sure enjoyed reading it. You ought to publish it someday." To his email I responded promptly with the words, "You're dead meat." I guess I should be thankful for my former good friend, Brad. Because of his suggestion I am sharing with you this personal journey—a journey that brought us back "home" to the United States.

Diapers and Politicians

Our fifteenth move as a family was back to the States. In a thousand years I never would have believed that I would be moving back to the United States. Very few days go by that I don't miss being overseas. Once we began getting settled in our new home just outside of Dallas, however, everything became clear. My wife began complaining of terrible pains in her pelvic area. Cancer was her first thought. The doctor gave my wife the diagnoses. My wife was pregnant—with twins. My wife is 10 hours older than I am. The day after her 40th birthday and on my 40th birthday we learned about the doubly exciting news. I began to count in my head: "Let's see. Four kids plus two more kids makes six kids—all ages 6 and under." By the time I emerged from my coma, the twins finally had arrived and the campaign for the U.S. Presidency between George

W. Bush and John Kerry was in full swing. In my entire life I never watched so much politics and changed so many dirty diapers at the same time. How are politicians like dirty diapers? You have to change them often and for the same reason.

I became fascinated by politics and politicians. I watched from beginning to end the Democratic and the Republican national conventions. I watched both the Presidential and Vice-Presidential debates. Why had I become so fascinated—even obsessed—with the political process? I think part of it had to do with the candidates being so different on their stances regarding various issues. The more I thought about it, however, the more I began to think maybe this had to do with the art of politics itself. If the truth were known, we would be amazed at how politicians say one thing and do another or say something that is far from the truth.

On *World News Tonight* Peter Jennings featured a segment called "Fact Check." He would examine the claims of Bush and Kerry in light of the facts. Many times both candidates were not even close in their claims about "the truth." Again I was amazed at how often and how much the truth was distorted. Both candidates were masters at distorting the facts in their favor.

Politicians—are they really who they say they are? Will they really do what they say they will do? Or, do they just tell us what we want to hear in order to win our vote of approval? I quickly moved to thinking about ourselves as Christians. I began asking the same questions. *Are we really who we say we are? Or, do we live to win the "vote of approval" from others?* Jesus has a word for those in the church who pretend and perform. Jesus has a word for those who say one thing and do another to win that vote of approval from others. He calls them "hypocrites."

Woe Is Me

In Jesus' day the original meaning of the word *hypocrite* referred to one who was an actor in a play. Hypocrites wore masks in playing their different roles. Hypocrites were those who put on a show for all to see. In public they were one way but in reality, behind closed doors, under their masks, they were totally different people. Jesus had much to say about hypocrites and hypocrisy in the church. In fact, more than 20 times in the New Testament, Jesus pronounces "woe" on those who pretend—the religious. You can see for yourself.

Get out your Bible and turn to Matthew 23:13-29. Seven times in these verses alone Jesus says "woe" to those who are insincere in their faith. But what does the word *woe* actually mean? In my opinion the word *woe* means judgment, condemnation, grief, and suffering. The most miserable person on earth is a Christian searching for happiness through what the world has to offer. I also like how John Walvoord, in his book, *The Bible Knowledge Commentary*, explains the word *woe.* According to Walvoord we safely can assume that God hates certain things. One of those things is fake Christianity.

The "Seriously Hyp" Checklist

I took the liberty of identifying some of the characteristics of hypocrisy, or pretending, that Jesus condemns in His Word. I could just have listed one-by-one the traits, but instead, I fashioned the list into a questionnaire entitled The "Seriously Hyp" Checklist. "Hyp", of course, is short for "hypocrisy." The checklist gives you an opportunity to familiarize yourself with the characteristics Jesus calls hypocrisy. At the same time you can determine if some of these traits are evident in your own life. Are you prone to pretend? Are you "seriously hyp"? Read through the characteristics listed below. Check the statements that describe you.

According to Jesus:

1. _____ Hypocrites believe that others exist to serve them, meet their needs, and make them happy. Their main question is, "What's in it for me?" They desire the best and most the world and the church have to offer.

2. _____ Hypocrites live for the praise of others. Recognition, praise, promotions, and success are most important. Character, integrity, and honesty are secondary.
3. _____ Hypocrites do good things to be seen by others. If nobody recognizes what they do, they call attention to themselves.
4. _____ Hypocrites love telling other people what to do and how to live. They are quick to give advice and easy answers to difficult questions.
5. _____ Hypocrites love to be recognized. They really like letters behind their names. They love titles—the longer, the better. They have nice offices, nice cars, and live in nice houses. They are successful, recognized, and respected.
6. _____ Hypocrites love to hear themselves talk. Their opinions, their prayers, their lessons, and/or their sermons are most important.
7. _____ Hypocrites go to church for what they can get out of it. They look forward to the end of the service so they can get home and get done what needs to be done. Worship is an event—not a lifestyle.
8. _____ Hypocrites have many excuses for not giving their full tithe to the church. Their desires are for their own financial prosperity. If they do give, they certainly want everyone to know about it and/or believe they have special rights and privileges because of their giving.
9. _____ Hypocrites judge others harshly, criticize, gossip, and complain. They don't give others the benefit of the doubt. They are quick to blame.
10. _____ Hypocrites make a huge deal out of small and insignificant matters. Others easily offend them over the most trivial matters. They are very sensitive and prideful.
11. _____ Hypocrites are those who have all the right answers. They know the right ways to act and the right

things to say. Their actions, however, do not match their beliefs—especially when no one else is watching.

12. _____ Hypocrites are success-driven. Their concern is for others to think well of them. Fear of rejection is a driving force.

13. _____ Hypocrites love to go on mission trips to prove how dedicated and devoted they are to God. They think mission trips make them a cut above other Christians even though rarely, if ever, have they seen another person trust Christ as a result of their own personal witness and testimony.

14. _____ Hypocrites are blinded by their own goodness and self-righteousness. They are the last to cry out, "God, have mercy on me, a sinner!" Instead, hypocrites hide their sin and pretend that everything is OK. They think, "Hey, in comparison to others, I'm doing pretty good."

15. _____ Hypocrites are beautiful to behold. They are model church members. They are the most religious, diligent-working, and most successful people in the church. Inside their hearts, behind closed doors, is a much different story.

16. _____ Hypocrites look over each one of these traits listed in this checklist and do not check one single blank. Hypocrites are experts at letting themselves slide. Instead, they think how good this checklist would be for others. They already have several people in mind.

17. _____ Hypocrites may not be genuine believers at all, even though they are among the "top" leaders in the church.

18. _____ Hypocrites are good people doing good things for good people to look good.

19 _____ Hypocrites do not realize that Jesus' greatest desire is to embrace them in the life-changing, transforming power of His love. Hypocrites simply have too much difficulty letting go of their control and admitting their desperate need for Christ.

So, how did you do? People ask, "Steve, how many blanks do I have to check if I'm prone to pretend?" If you checked five or more, I am glad you are reading this book. If you checked 10 or more, you are "seriously hyp." The first time I went through the list, I checked eight of the blanks. Jesus said, "Steve, woe to you! You are the one who needs to get down on your knees and cry out for mercy." I was so convicted. I remember praying and asking God's forgiveness for my hypocrisy. To be perfectly honest, at times, I'm still amazed at how much I desire the applause and approval of others.

I'll never forget when, on national television, Sally Field revealed her desperate need for applause and approval. She clutched her Oscar for the 1984 movie *Places in the Heart* and gently placed the trophy to her cheek as she tearfully exclaimed, "I can't deny the fact you like me—right now, you like me." When this innermost desire to be accepted and liked was revealed on that award-winning day, Field was mocked, criticized, brutalized, and trampled under foot. The truth is, the overwhelming majority of us are desperate to be loved and accepted. We hate it. We hide it and mercilessly condemn it when we see it in others. But why? Why are we so desperate for love, approval, and acceptance that we would sacrifice anything good and godly—especially our character and integrity?

They Both Look the Same to Me

I already mentioned our twins and probably will mention them a few more times before this book ends. I never dreamed they would be so much work. I had thought that rearing two at one time would be about twice as much work as would rearing one child at a time. I was wrong. I discovered rearing twins was 10 times as much time, trouble, energy, and effort. I can't tell you how many times I laid awake at night and prayed, "Lord, I'm not going to make it. It's simply too much." Most nights I was so tired, I called the twins, "This One" and "That One." I'd ask, "Do you want me to feed This One? Do you want me to change That One? Do you want me to burp This One? Do you want me to hold That One?" Sometimes my wife asked, "Could you feed Jordan?" or "Could you change Julia?" My response always was, "Now, which one is which? They both look the same to me."

Such was the case after arriving back in America after living overseas. I couldn't tell the difference between the world and the church. This seemed much more obvious to me after I was away for several years. Look at the following statistics as reported by Maranatha Life (*www.maranathalife.com/lifeline/stats.htm*) and Family Safe Media (*www.familysafemedia.com/pornography_statistics.html*):

> Among evangelical Christians, internet pornography and sexual immorality are among the top reasons for the dissolution of their families and departure from ministry and the church. Revenues from the pornography industry in America are greater than are the revenues generated by the professional football, basketball, and baseball industries combined. The pornography industry in America receives more revenue than do CBS, NBC, and ABC networks combined.
>
> A confidential survey over the past three years revealed that 70 percent of Christian leaders and pastors struggle with sexual sin and sexual addiction.
>
> Eight-eight percent of children in evangelical churches leave the church by the time they are age 18 and never return.
>
> Approximately two-thirds of the members of Southern Baptist churches do not attend church on a regular basis. (My comment: And that's just one denomination!)
>
> Fifteen hundred pastors leave the ministry each month because of moral failure, spiritual burnout, exhaustion, or contention in their churches.

Fifty percent of pastors are so discouraged that they would leave the ministry if they could but have no other way of making a living.

Eighty-five percent of pastors said their greatest problem is that they are sick and tired of dealing with problem people, such as disgruntled elders, deacons, worship leaders, worship teams, board members, and associate pastors. Ninety percent said the most difficult thing about ministry is dealing with uncooperative people.

Eighty percent of pastors' spouses believe their spouse is overworked.

Eighty percent of pastors' spouses wish their spouse would choose another profession.

The majority of pastors' wives surveyed said that the most destructive event that has occurred in their marriage and family occurred the day they entered the ministry.

More than half of all committed laymen and pastors have had some kind of inappropriate involvement—either emotional or physical—with a woman outside of marriage.

Close to 40 percent of pastors surveyed confessed to have been involved in inappropriate sexual behavior with some one in the church.

More than half of men involved with Promise Keepers reported to have viewed pornography in the past week.

George Barna (*www.barna.org*), one of my favorite Christian researchers of all time, reported that the divorce rate actually is higher among born-again believers than among atheists and agnostics. He went on to state that Southern Baptists have the highest divorce rate of all denominations. Barna's Program Director Meg Flammang said she would love to be able to report differences in attitude and behavior between Christians and non-Christians, but research simply does not support this assumption.

Holly Peters has more startling statistics. In her article, "Evangelicals on the Decline" in *The Biola Connection* (pp. 9-15), she reported that only five percent of people in America are truly, born-again, evangelical Christians. The Barna Group was much more positive and gracious with its statistics. Barna's research group reported that seven percent of Americans are evangelical, born-again Christians. They also reported that 75 percent of mainline, Protestant church members believe they can earn their way to heaven.

What do these statistics mean? They mean that the overwhelming majority of Americans who think they are Christians are not really saved at all. The statistics also mean the vast majority of church members are simply going through the motions—pretending, while fooling themselves into believing they are living lives that honor God. Today, unlike any time in the history of our nation, our culture and the church are one and the same.

My questions, however, still remain. What's going on? Why are we no longer who we say we are as Christians? Why are we so busy pretending, performing, impressing, and striving to succeed? Why are we willing to sacrifice everything for love? The answers to these questions are the purpose for writing this book.

On a personal note…

Were you as shocked as I was by the statistics? The first time I read through them, I wept. Even though I lived out of the country for several years, I still was shocked. Simply recognizing the problems and asking the questions is not enough. Discovering why a problem exists and identifying suggestions for dealing with it is important. Before you move forward, please read the next section, "You're in the Spotlight", to reflect on some personal questions.

You're in the Spotlight

After each chapter you'll find a section entitled "You're in the Spotlight" It is an opportunity for God to shed light into the hidden areas of your life. Scripture states, "Everyone who does evil hates the light, and will not come into the light for fear that his deeds will be exposed. But whoever lives by the truth comes into the light, so that it may be seen plainly that what he has done has been done through God" (John 3:20-21). Sharing your story is of utmost importance when you deal with matters such as pretending, hiding, and hypocrisy. Throughout this book I plan on being open and brutally honest with you. Being open and honest is important for you, as well. Whenever secrets exist, hiding always occurs. What we hide is what makes and keeps us unhealthy. Take an opportunity to "step into the light" as you reflect on the following questions.

1. Are you prone to pretend? Which characteristics on the checklist were most descriptive of you?

2. How would you rate yourself on the following scale?

1	5	10
I definitely am a hypocrite	I'd like to move toward a more authentic Christian life	I live an authentic Christian life

3. How did you react after reading the statistics regarding the condition of today's church? How is the hypocrisy you see in the church reflected in your own life and vice-versa? Is your Christian life reflecting God's glory, or is it self-glorifying? Explain your answer.

Stepping into God's Light

After you reflect on and answer the questions in the section entitled, "You're in the Spotlight", we will have the privilege of praying together. I look forward to traveling on this journey with you. Seeking the Lord step-by-step on the way is important. Before you move to the next chapter, take an opportunity to pray and commit our time to Him.

Heavenly Father,

As my new friend and I begin this journey together, the first thing I want to do is to pray. Jesus, thank You for who You are. You are Lord. You are Lord of all but intimately involved in every detail of our lives. You love us with a love that never changes—no matter what. One of your greatest desires is for us to have an open, honest, and genuine relationship with You. Heavenly Father, forgive us if we are counted among the statistics in this chapter. Forgive us if we are numbered with those who call themselves Christians but who react, respond, and live exactly as the rest of the world does.

As this dear reader and I walk through this material, allow us to catch a glimpse of who You are. Allow us to see ourselves for who we really are as Your children. Through this process, grow us in a deeper walk and relationship with You and others. Heavenly Father, thank you, once again, for this precious one—this dear reader. Now Lord, we turn our attention to You as we move to the next chapter and begin to explore some of the reasons we hide and pretend—starting with the introduction of shame.

We pray in the Name of Jesus. Amen.

Chapter 2

A Star Is Born

My disgrace is before me all day long, and my face is covered with shame (Ps. 44:15).

Whenever something to hide exists in one's life, so does shame. If guilt is feeling sorry for what we do, shame is feeling sorry for who we are. Shame kills us at the core of who we are with the lie, "I'm not worthy to be loved." If shame is at the heart of our hiding, then how does shame occur? This is yet another great question. In our next chapters, beginning with the first reason for shame—heart-breaking and devastating circumstances—we will address the answers to this question. As you will see, this is how I personally was introduced to shame.

Lights, Camera, Action!

He takes center stage. He becomes the star. He is a dastardly villain. He is tall and slender. He is dressed in black with matching black leather boots and a flowing black cape. His beady eyes complement his twisted moustache. His laugh is deep and evil. He is merciless. He punishes at every opportunity. He is critical. He is controlling. He is manipulative. He is a liar. He is a brutal opponent. He proves to be the mighty "Internal Destroyer" of all that is true and innocent. His name is "Shame." His appearance on the scene is devastating.

Introducing Shame

The steps leading up to my personal introduction to shame really began the first day I stepped onto the campus of Saint Bernadette Private Catholic School down in the bayous of Southern Louisiana—way down South. We moved to Houma, LA, about 15 miles from the Gulf of Mexico. My attending a Catholic school seemed strange, especially since at age 6 I had been baptized as a Lutheran. (Ultimately, at age 12, I was baptized as a full-fledged Southern Baptist and was rebaptized in a Baptist church when I was 16.) I definitely was a strange mix. This reminds me of the woman who went to the post office to buy stamps for her Christmas cards. "What denomination?" asked the clerk. "Oh, good heavens! Are things this bad?" replied the woman. "Well, give me 50 Baptist and 50 Catholic ones."

Even at the ripe old age of 8, I knew that I was bordering on heresy by stepping onto Catholic soil as a Lutheran. Being from Texas, I probably was bordering on heresy stepping foot into Louisiana. The first inhabitants that I contacted in this strange, New World were nuns. I remember thinking, "Wow, nuns are really big." Sister Mary Edmund was the biggest person I ever had seen. She was dressed in a white robe, black habit, and a string of rosary beads with a dangling crucifix that could anchor the biggest of ships in the fiercest of storms. Sister Mary was enough to put the fear of God into any 8-year-old, Texas-Lutheran-Protestant. As we toured the school, she whistled a little tune—*Amazing Grace.*

Amazing grace was exactly what the student needed who Sister Mary caught talking in the lunch line. I heard a story about a Catholic lunch line. In the cafeteria of a Catholic school, the children were lined up for lunch. At the head of the line was a large pile of apples. The nun made a note and placed it in front of the apples. The note read: "Take only one; God is watching." Further down the cafeteria line was a large pile of chocolate-chip cookies. One of the boys had written a note of his own. The note he placed in front of the cookies read: "Take all you want; God is watching the apples." Now, I am not a lip reader, but I swear that I saw this student making things right with his Maker. Sister Mary left me and marched straight toward him. She ultimately made a dead stop right at his side. With her left hand the good sister proceeded to grab the boy's right ear and pick him up by that facial extremity until he was standing on the tips of his toes. Deep into the drum of his ear and into the depths of his mind she whispered, "Please, don't ever talk in the lunch line again. Thank you." From that memorable day forward I was the most well behaved, obedient, respectful, Texan, Lutheran, Protestant, and now God-fearing, Catholic boy that South Louisiana and St. Bernadette Private School ever had seen.

A Gift and a Curse

After a few short months of observation, the good sisters told my parents that I was what they called a "gifted" child—academically. I took some aptitude tests. As a result of my scores, my nun friends decided that I needed to skip a grade in order to better accommodate my academic needs. So, the very next day, I made the big jump from third grade to fifth grade. When I sized up some of the boys in my new class, I reasoned that I not only was going to have to do my own homework but also some of theirs—maybe even some of the girls' as well—or give out a ton of lunch money. As I later would find out, skipping fourth grade would turn out to be one of the biggest curses in my entire life. The later repercussions of this one event profoundly would impact my entire life—even to this day.

First, Some Great Days

Writing that being gifted academically was a curse for me does seem a shame. This was not a curse for me as long as I lived in Louisiana and attended a private school. The importance of excelling academically was supported and encouraged at St. Bernadette. I did not have to worry about being teased or harassed and ultimately abused for being smart. Sometimes I wonder how different my life would have been if I would have continued in private schools where the Bible was taught, where we prayed in our classes, where academics and right behavior and morals were emphasized, and where I never was afraid to go to school. Later, I forever would learn the true definitions of fear, terror, and trauma in school. I look back on my days at St. Bernadette Catholic School down in the bayous of Houma, LA, as being some of the best days of my entire life. I was loved. I was accepted. I was at peace. I loved those nuns. I sure hated to say goodbye.

Back to Texas

My dad's job took us back to Texas—South Texas—Victoria to be exact. "Victoria"—just the thought of the place still creates terror in the deepest part of my soul. Even now, almost 30 years later, when I hear the name, I get the same nauseous feelings down in the deepest pit of my stomach. Victoria was, and still is, the very definition of hell for me. If Victoria, TX, was hell for me, then Satan himself lived and reigned in my seventh-grade gym class. If Satan had a name, his name was Gary.

I was at a new school with new rules. Unfortunately, the main rule was the survival of the fittest and strongest. I already was at a huge disadvantage since I was a year younger than everyone else was. It showed. I was not fit; I was certainly not strong. If the truth were known, I was more like Pee Wee Herman incarnate. As far as my secondary sex characteristics kicking into gear in my life, I was not even sure that my primary sex characteristics were working. I was small in every way. I was underdeveloped in every way. I had no body hair other than that on my head. I spoke two or three octaves higher than all the guys and than some of the girls. I was short and skinny.

I quickly learned that ample body hair, muscles, height, and a deep voice were the most important qualities to have if you wanted to survive seventh-grade gym class in public school in Victoria, TX.

As you have probably already surmised, Pee Wee did not have much hope in hell.

Getting Beat

I remember the volleyball game as though it were yesterday. Even now, as I write, I have huge regrets. If only I had kept my big mouth shut. To this day, I never will figure out what caused me to do it. So, what happened? While playing volleyball, I accidentally ran into one of the bigger boys— actually, the biggest boy. He pushed me to the ground and angrily said, "Watch out, you little punk!" For some strange and unknown reason, I spoke. I never spoke. I had no friends, so I had no reason to speak. I was a non-entity. But that day, I responded. I said (rather sheepishly, I might add), "Stick it, Gary!" To this day, I cannot figure out how in the world those words escaped my mouth.

After I uttered those infamous words, I saw Gary's face contort and twist into the essence of total evil and rage. I actually waited for his head to turn around and for the pea soup to spew. He replied, "We will see about that, punk." I think he may have been watching too many Clint Eastwood movies. After gym class, when I returned to my locker, four guys including Gary cornered me and began taking turns punching me, kicking me, spitting on me, and laughing at me. After the beating, I was dragged into the showers where "the cherry" was put on top—snot-laden spit, followed by ripe urine and high fives to end the ritual. The whole experience was painful and humiliating. It was devastating, if you want to know the honest truth. After the beating was over, I stayed in a little ball in the corner of the shower and cried. After everyone left, I showered, went to my locker, put on my school clothes, and went to class. I was filled with absolute shame. The beatings continued every day for an entire year. I suffered in silence. I told no one. I had no one to tell. I had no friends. No one even knew—or cared—that I existed.

On a personal note...

Thirty years later, I sit here and reflect on those days. I am filled with the same shame and heartache. Day after day not one person helped as the sounds of the beating and my cries echoed throughout the locker room. I experienced up-close and personal what the term "learned helplessness" was all about. Three decades later, I see in my mind and in my heart that little, humiliated boy. I want to help him, hug him, clean him up, and let him know that everything will be okay.

Funny What You Remember

I guess even nobodies—the losers, the forgotten, and the hated—have their limit. I surprised even myself. Amazingly enough, one day I gathered all the courage and strength I could gather. I summoned all the inner strength a beaten, hopeless, shamed, 125-pound, 12-year-old boy could muster and took the brave and courageous step to finally tell someone about my living hell. I stepped into my coach's office. I did not know too much about coaches. I certainly did not know anything about my coach. He always was in his office reading his sports page. I did learn from the *Late Show with David Letterman* what coaches are not supposed to say during halftime. Are you ready? Here are five things a coach should not say at halftime:

"If you don't mind, I'm going to leave now to beat the traffic."

"Who's winning?"

"Enough strategy. Let me tell you about my Amway products."

"They may have the talent, size, and athleticism, but we've got the headbands!"

"It's not over until . . . who am I kidding? It's over!"

I took a deep breath and marched into my coach's office. Funny what you remember during the heartbreaking and humiliating times of life. My P.E. coach reminded me of the comedian Jonathan Winters. He was the spittin' image. So, we'll just call my coach Coach Winters. I stood and he sat at his desk obviously perturbed that I was interrupting his daily reading of the sports section. I completely unloaded. I shared the whole, devastating story. As I told the story, I began to weep and to shake uncontrollably. I was humiliated and ashamed to share finally what had gone on in gym class every day for the past year. I felt helpless and weak. Coach Winters did not say a word. From time to time I would catch his eyes glancing down at the sports section. Must have been a great article. Finally, after what seemed like an eternity of silence, he stated, "Sorry. I can't do anything. You will just have to take it like a man. Go get dressed. You'll be late for class." He returned to reading his paper. I remember thinking, "You've got to be kidding. That's it? I don't care if you do look like Jonathan Winters. This is *not* funny."

In utter hopelessness and helplessness, I turned away. When I turned to walk out of the coach's office, to my left I noticed a huge window spanning the length of the boys' locker room and the coach's office. I never had noticed it before. I guess it was so the coach could make sure everything was OK in the locker room. Guess he had been reading the sports section every day for the past year. That day, however, a group of individuals were looking into the coach's office through that same glass but from the other side. There they were—all of my accusers—my abusers staring through the window watching the whole time, laughing at me, and mocking me, then pretending to cry as I was. They stood there with faces of victory, with faces of pride, with faces of self-satisfaction. I never will forget the looks on their faces. Funny what you remember during the heartbreaking and humiliating times.

It was the most humiliating moment in all of my life. After Coach Winters shared his words of wisdom, support, and empathy, I returned—completely dejected and defeated—to the locker room. The same four guys, including Gary, waited for me. They cornered me and began taking turns punching me, kicking me, spitting on me, laughing at me, and tearing my gym clothes while dragging me to the shower for the grand finale-—the golden shower. I remember hearing one of the guys say while he laughed, "I've been saving this up for you, boy." After the beating was over, once again I gathered myself into a little ball in the corner and cried. I prayed an unanswered prayer for death. After everyone left, I showered, went to my locker, put on my clothes, and went to class.

This daily ritual continued for another year, with the exception of five miraculous days. For five days a boy named Mike took up for me. He told my group of abusers that he would rip them to shreds if any of them touched me. For five days they left me alone. Then, without warning, Mike moved to another city. After those five glorious days, the beatings continued. I was shocked that someone would take up for me. I had absolutely no friends. No one would dare speak to me. No one would associate with me. But for some reason, this person—this angel in disguise—stood up for me. Somehow after that the beatings did not seem so bad anymore. Don't ask why. So, Mike, wherever you are, thanks for those five miraculous days!

Two Wrongs Don't Make a Right

I don't know whether this development happened because of the beginning of puberty, stress, or the terror of going to gym class every day, but my face began to break out. That's right. I had pimples—big ones. As a result, my abusers added new names to their list. In addition to my regular names of "wimp" and "sissy", "pimple-face" and "pizza-face" were added to the list. The name-calling cut deeper into my heart and soul than did any physical abuse. I just wanted the humiliating names to stop. Then, for some strange and unknown reason (a reason that I still wonder about to this day), I made the second biggest mistake in my life. I tried to cover up my blemishes with some stolen makeup from my mom's bathroom drawer. Obviously, I did not do a very good job with the application. I remember one person in my science class yelling at the top of his lungs, "Look! The pimple-faced wimp is wearing makeup!"

From that day forward, I officially was labeled a “girl”, “feminine”, “gay”, a “homosexual”, and a “fag”, along with many other profane names too horrible to mention. The do-it-yourself Extreme Makeover was not such a good idea after all.

News traveled quickly around the school. Now my abuse extended beyond gym class. Popular, “beautiful” girls (beautiful in appearance) approached me as I walked to class and pretended to hold my hand and kiss me on the cheek. “Look, I’m a lesbian,” they yelled out. Can you believe it? Girls even made fun of me. Could things get any worse? Their boyfriends would push me, knock my books out of my hands, or knee me in both thighs and create huge bruises. They would say, “Stay away from my girl, lesbian.” They would hit me on my arms and create large bruises. They would push me into the lockers and push me to the floor. This was great entertainment for them. This occurred during seventh grade, eighth grade, and part of ninth grade. It was an absolute nightmare. It was a nightmare I thought never would end. I prayed for death. I never told anyone. I was too frightened. I was too ashamed.

Every person is said to have his or her breaking point. I obviously reached mine. I literally heard something break within my soul. Something within the deepest part of my heart and soul was shattered. At the shattering point a new substance seeped down into crevices of my broken heart. I later identified that stagnating ooze as shame. Shame replaced hope. Shame invaded my heart and made a nice comfortable home. I once heard someone describe the difference between shame and guilt. Guilt is feeling sorry for what you do. Shame is feeling sorry for who you are. Shame now resided in the deepest part of my heart and soul. With hope gone, shame’s lies crept down deep into my broken heart. I believed what they said about me. At the core of who I was, I accepted as truth their devastating words. I was not a man. I was ugly. I was disgusting. I was unworthy of love and deserved to be alone and punished. Insecurity, inadequacy, shame, and fear haunted me in the depths of my soul.

> ***On a personal note…***
>
> *I guess I should say something personal at this point, but thinking of anything to say is difficult. Kids can be really mean. I read the story I just told you and have to admit that the memories still cut like a knife. I would like to think that I am over all of that. I'm fine. I'm strong. It's nothing. But that's not the case. I did rewrite a favorite childhood saying. I like my version much better.*
>
> *"Sticks and stones may break my bones,*
> *But words can hurt forever."*

Why Didn't You Tell Anybody?

I know what you are asking: "Why didn't you tell anybody? Why didn't you tell your parents—somebody?" If I had told my parents, they would have done everything possible to rescue me. The power of shame is deceitful. Part of the lie of shame for me was that I believed that everything happening to me was somehow my fault. In other words I was rejected and abused because something was wrong with me. The nature of shame is to hide. Whenever shame occurs, hiding also occurs. Adam and Eve experienced this; I certainly did. I chose to pretend that everything was OK. Once again, whenever shame is, pretending and performing also are there. I chose to hide and to avoid the risk of further rejection and heartache. I chose to suffer in silence. Trust me—if I knew then what I know now, I would have dealt with things a little bit differently. OK, I would have dealt with things A LOT differently.

One thing I would have done differently was to tell my parents. More than any other question—after people read this book—they'll ask me, "Steve, what do your parents say about what happened? Have you shared this story with your parents?" Wow! These are really personal questions, but they are good ones. After 30 years, I shared with my parents this story. This is what they had to say. I love and respect my dad more than any man on earth. He said: "Steve, first of all, I would like to tell you that I am heartbroken over what happened to you in junior high. I do wish you would have told me. Second, I would like to say that you are a godly, Christian man. You are a real picture of what a Christian man is supposed to be. No dad has ever been prouder of a son than I am of you. Don't ever forget how much I love you. Remember, I am always here for you—no matter what."

My mom has stood by me through thick and thin. She always has been there for me and still is. My mom's words: "Steve, if you are ever in trouble again and don't tell me, I'm going to spank your little behind. I don't care if you are a grown man. Now, get washed up for dinner."

You're in the Spotlight

Once again, you have an opportunity to allow God to shed His light into the "hidden" areas of your life. I always have heard the sayings, "What we hide is what makes us unhealthy," or "Our secrets are what make us sick."

Whenever you deal with matters such as shame, pride, and performance, sharing your story is of utmost importance. So many secrets accompany shame. So much hiding accompanies hypocrisy. Take an opportunity to "step into the light" as you reflect on the following questions:

1. Shame was described as a dastardly villain—a robber of all that is good and true. How would you describe shame?

2. How was shame born in your life? How have the people or events in your past contributed to your feelings of shame?

3. How has shame distorted your beliefs about who you are (i.e. your self-worth, self-image, value)?

4. What role did secrets play in your life growing up? What role do secrets play in your life now? What are your thoughts about

the following statements: "What we hide is what makes us unhealthy", or "Our secrets are what make us sick"?

5. If our secrets make us sick and the truth sets us free, who is a trusted Christian friend, pastor, or Christian counselor with whom you can share regarding your personal battle with shame, pride, and secret sins? Be careful with this step. Test the waters before you reach out and trust just anyone. Begin praying now that the Lord might lead you to the right person or persons.

Stepping into God's Light

Heavenly Father,

Once again, we stand before You and recognize You as Lord. You love us and care for us even in the most devastating of times. We confess that in the heartbreaking times we are tempted to doubt. We are tempted to question and ask, "God, where are You? Don't You care?" The Accuser, Satan, would love for us to believe such lies. When we believe You don't care, we turn our backs on You and strive to meet our own needs. Father, You promised we would have difficulties in this world. Remind us that You use the difficult circumstances and difficult people of life to deepen our walk and grow our faith in You.

Father, guide us as we continue to look at shame and the reasons we hide. Shame can creep into our hearts and lives as a result of the heartbreaking circumstances of life. It can lock us in a prison of fear, insecurity, and inadequacy. Guide us as we examine the next birthplace of shame—rigid and religious households.

We pray in the Name of Jesus. Amen.

Chapter 3

Image Is Everything

Peter and the other apostles replied: "We must obey God rather than men!" (Acts 5:29).

Shame pervaded my innermost being—my heart, my mind, and my soul. There I was in the shower in the corner, with my accusers urinating on me, spitting on me, and cursing me. The greatest tragedy was that I began to believe what they said about me. As a result, shame was born. I embraced the lies of my accusers. I traded the truth for lies. I accepted the lie that I was absolutely worthless. This lie found its home in the deepest part of my heart. We hide and pretend because of shame. We addressed the first reason for the birth of shame. Shame can be born through devastating circumstances and heartbreaking circumstances. Now let's address a second birthplace of shame—behind the walls of rigid and religious households.

Lights, Camera, Action!

A new character enters the scene. He springs to life in the heart of a closed, rigid, and religious household where appearances are of utmost importance and image is everything. He is strong and problem-free. Everything always is OK for him. He has the right words to say and knows the right things to do. Behind the image, however, he is filled with resentment, rebellion, selfishness, and secret sins. He looks for opportunities to sneak around and do exactly what he wants to do. His name is "Compliance." To avoid punishment, criticism, and rejection he conforms outwardly to those who are in control. When no one else is looking, the picture is much different. Deep down is the desire to do whatever he wants whenever he wants, no matter what anybody else says.

The Hug of Freedom

One of my favorite shows of all time is *Braveheart.* After William Wallace's betrayal, with his two closest friends watching in the midst of an angry and hostile crowd, the executioner strapped Wallace to the gallows after tremendous torture. All this brave warrior had to do was to swear allegiance to the King of England. Swearing allegiance to the king would ensure him a quick and painless death, but the character that actor Mel Gibson portrayed would not submit. As he was sliced open and his entrails pulled out, he yelled at the top of his lungs, "Freedom!" while he passed from this life to meet his wife in the next. His death inspired the warrior-poets of Scotland to win their freedom.

A missionary who would not "swear allegiance" to hiding and hypocrisy any more equally inspired me with his story of freedom. As director of pastoral care and counseling for missionaries serving in Central and Eastern Europe, I had the privilege of talking to one of the most successful missionaries on the field. Outwardly he was attractive. He was a head taller than everybody else—blond, popular, married, a parent, and a respected leader on the field. What surprised me and shocked me were his beliefs about who he was "underneath the surface." He said things such as, "I'm unworthy of love and deserve to be punished. I hate myself. I'm a failure." I never will forget Tom's story. He told me, "If my story might help anybody else, please feel free to share it." This is what he shared:

> My family has its secrets. To even tell you what I am going to tell you is breaking a major family rule—never share your secrets. My dad never was at home when I was growing up. He was home, but things didn't seem that way growing up. As I look back, he was home every night. He

just got in late. He was tired. He would eat, watch TV, and then go to bed. He was gone the following morning before I woke up. He worked. He worked like no one I ever had known. He was dedicated to his job and his employers. He also was motivated. His desire and motivation was to give his children all the things he didn't have when he was growing up. I learned much later that being a good provider was his way of showing love. If this was the case, then no one loved me more than my dad did. I see that now. I guess I was most angry at my dad because he was unaware of what was going on at home when he was away at work. Every day, after school, I would have to go home and face my mom. I don't know if maybe my mom and dad were going through difficult times. Maybe it was partly because my mom was the child of an abusive, alcoholic father. But I do remember getting beaten by my mother with a belt, with her hand, or sometimes with things that happened to be available. The physical punishment wasn't what caused the greatest damage. I was a pretty strong-willed and stubborn child. I probably deserved a good spanking most of the time. The things my mother said more than the physical punishment caused much damage and pain for me. I never will forget some of her devastating sayings:

- You never will amount to anything.
- I wish you never had been born.
- You never do anything right.
- Can't you do anything right?
- Shut up that crying before I give you something to cry about.
- I'm going to beat you until you bleed.
- You are so stupid.
- You don't deserve to live.
- You never will amount to anything.
- I wish you never had been born.

> Because of those painful messages from my mom I literally have killed myself as a Christian trying to prove to her, to God, and especially to myself that I am worthy of love. I am so tired. I am so exhausted. I can't take it another day. I am so tired of pretending.

I listened to his story. My heart broke right along with his. After he finished sharing, we both stood up at the same time. I reached out to give him a hug. I happen to be a hugger, but I was shocked. He didn't hug me back. His arms hung limp at his side. I never had experienced anything like it before. After we parted ways, I worried about him all night long. The next day I saw him. He looked completely different. He was filled with joy. It was an amazing transformation. He talked to me about "the hug." He said that he was so surprised to find a listening ear, care, compassion, and a warm hug after sharing his story that he did not know how to respond to the hug. He said, "For the first time in my life I feel free. I no longer have to hide my secret." He gave me a hug. As he walked off , he cried out, "Freedom!" Talk about a brave heart.

Giving Birth at Home

How is shame born in religious and rigid households? Birth is something about which I happen to know a few things. My wife and I have friends who are missionaries with five kids. Three of their kids were born at home. One of their kids was born in the bathtub. A fellow professor, who is a friend, has five kids. His wife gave birth to their five kids at home with a midwife present. Now, I realize that we are crazy for having six kids, but I assure you, all of them were born in the hospital—even when one of the hospitals was in Prague, Czech Republic.

I consider myself and my wife to be what I call "birth" experts. While I waited for my wife to give birth to our twins, in the waiting room I met four expectant fathers while their wives were in labor. The nurse entered and told the first man, "Congratulations! You're the father of twins!" "What a coincidence!" the man exclaimed. "I work for the Twin Star Enterprise!" The nurse returned a short while later and told the second expectant father, "You are the father of triplets!" "Wow, what a coincidence!" he replied. "I work for the 3M Corporation!" When the nurse appeared again, she told the third expectant father that his wife had given birth to quadruplets. "Another coincidence! I work for the Four Seasons Hotel!" At that point the fourth guy fainted. When he finally revived, the others asked, "What's wrong?" "What's wrong?" He exclaimed, "I work for 7UP!"

As a birth expert, I want to talk about how shame is born in religious households. In other words, how is hypocrisy conceived at home? What type of family environment contributes to pretending and performance? What are the characteristics of parents who breed children who strive to be the best they can be in order to earn love? Let's begin answering this question by seeing how you score on the following "Playing House" Checklist.

"Playing House" Checklist

Are you part of a family in which image is everything? Within your own family are you hiding and pretending? What secret sins are you hiding even from those who are closest to you? Is your family different behind closed doors than in church on Sunday mornings? Are you just "playing house"? Take out a pencil or pen. First, read through the following characteristics and determine which characteristics describe your current, immediate family. Place a check mark in the first blank for each applicable statement. Then, if you are a parent, go back through the checklist a second time. In the second blank place an "X" if the statements below describe how you were reared in your family of origin. Good luck. I'll meet you at the end.

1. _____ Good enough is never good enough. Our home has frequent criticism, frequent lectures about how things are sup-

posed to be, and one-sided communication. Expressing your opinion doesn't do any good _____.

2. _____ Things are black and white, right and wrong. Expectations are really high. Things must be done a certain way _____.

3. _____ As punishment, love is withdrawn. When things aren't done the right way, outbursts of anger, frustration, and harsh criticism occur _____.

4. _____ Anger is used to force compliance. Threats are used to force compliance. "If you don't do this, you're gonna get it" is just one example of how threats are used to force compliance _____.

5. _____ Life really is busy. The family has little time for fun, relaxation, and laughing. The atmosphere of the home is serious. The majority of downtime, if any, is spent in front of the television _____.

6. _____ Expectations are unreasonable. Meeting expectations and feeling accepted almost is impossible _____.

7. _____ Appearance is of utmost importance. A vast difference exists between what goes on in public (i.e., in church) and what goes on in private behind closed doors. One could be looking at two separate families _____.

8. _____ An absence of prayer, devotion, and Bible study exists in the home. A blessing at mealtimes may have been offered, but beyond that, not much spiritual occurs. Spouses don't pray together on a regular basis. Parents don't pray on a regular basis with their kids _____.

9. _____ The family provides little opportunity to question. Anger is a feeling that must not be expressed. Back talk is punishable by death, or worse—the withdrawal of love and approval _____.

10. _____ Communication is almost non-existent. The quality of communication is poor. Very rarely is the TV turned off, the computer unplugged, or the phone turned off. Work is brought home in the evenings. Work takes priority over the family _____.

11. _____ Children are compared with each other. They often hear, "If only you could be like so and so." In other words, to get attention, you must be the best or stand out _____.
12. _____ The message is communicated (verbally or non-verbally), "Because you do bad, you are bad." The message is not communicated, "I love you. You are valuable no matter what your behavior" _____.
13. _____ The family has favorite household sayings such as, "Can't you do anything right?" "How many times do I have to tell you?" "You'll never learn." "You're impossible." "I wish you never had been born." "You'll never amount to anything." "Don't you ever listen?" "As long as you live in this house, that's how it is." "You'll never get it." "You don't appreciate me and all I do" _____.
14. _____ Spouses fight and argue. They do so in front of the kids. The husband and/or the wife are blatantly angry and controlling—not in public but behind closed doors. The atmosphere of the home is one of fear and insecurity _____.
15. _____ The parents are religious. They go to church on a regular basis. They are deacons, Sunday-school teachers, pastors, or choir members. They are much different at home _____.
16. _____ One or both parents are plagued by shame or deep feelings of insecurity, inadequacy, and failure. This ensures that shame is passed on to future generations _____.
17. _____ The family has plenty of secrets. The family is unwilling to reach out for help when necessary _____.

So, how did you do? Would you characterize your household as a rigid or religious household? If you are a parent, how did the way in which you were reared compare with how you parent your own children? Do you see a connection? Again, if you checked five or more statements, then you probably are wise to be reading this book. If you marked eight or more, then you have some serious problems. I remember the first time I read through this "Playing House Checklist." I was convicted. I remember praying and asking God's forgiveness for my hypocrisy. I had to admit that I was much different at home than I was at church. I was much different at work than I was at home. If I had treated others at work like I treated my own family, I would have been fired. I went to each of my family members and asked for their forgiveness.

Homeland Insecurity

I hear what you are saying, "OK. Now, I know a few characteristics of rigid and religious households. How do these households contribute and even cause shame?" The answer is that kids in these types of homes must strive to be their best and do their best in order to earn love, approval, and acceptance. At the same time, children in these types of households must strive to be their best and do their best in order to avoid criticism, rejection, and punishment. Tragically, those kids who are the most sensitive and caring are those who suffer the most. Children are a great barometer of what goes on in the home. What goes on in a rigid and religious households, behind closed doors, is nothing short of devastating.

Here's a bit more explanation. In religious homes, life is black and white. In reality, people are gray. In religious homes, life is a list of do's and don'ts. In reality, Christianity is a loving relationship with Christ and with others. In religious homes, doing right is the key to being right. Actually we can't do enough "right" things to be made right before God.

I constantly have deeply religious Christians ask me, "What do you mean? Nothing is more important than doing right and being right!" Of course, they never listen to my response. Their inability to listen is a huge part of their problem. I try to explain anyway. I try to explain that **rules and regulations without the relationship always breed rebellion and resentment.**

I try to explain that being right and doing right are not what make us right. What Christ has done for us and what He can do through us and in us are most important. But dogmatic, rigid Christians seldom are open to listen. Saying something to them really doesn't do much good.

In rigid and religious households, appearances are of utmost importance. Such families have the demand for compliance, the demand for goodness, the demand to be the best, and the unwillingness to embrace fears, weaknesses, failures, and mistakes. The goal is to be the perfect, all-American, Christian family. Expectations are unreasonable, unrealistic, and unhealthy. Individuals are not respected. Feelings are not respected. Differing opinions are not respected. When individuals are not respected, they are not loved. When individuals are not loved, tremendous damage to self-worth, self-esteem, and personal value exist. This type of secretive, rigid, religious, and closed family atmosphere always is devastating. The uncompromising stand for what is right and true without the balance of grace, love, mercy, forgiveness, and acceptance always is devastating. As a result, shame is born. Whenever shame exists, hiding and pretending also exist.

Finally, and most devastatingly, in rigid and religious homes love is withdrawn for failure to comply and meet expectations. Constant criticism, lectures, outbursts of anger, demands, and other forms of punishment are used to force compliance. Love and acceptance are withdrawn whenever a family member does not do what he or she is "supposed to do." Family members learn a devastating message: "I must earn love, approval, and acceptance." In rigid and religious homes the desire to please, to meet expectations, and to earn love work together to create a tremendous fear of failure and rejection.

Perfectionism is born. Why? Because, once love is earned, it must be kept. The desire and drive to be perfect and maintain perfection are the keys to earning love and maintaining love. In this type of conditional environment the ultimate belief about oneself is that "I am not valuable for who I am. I only am valuable when I do what I am supposed to do." As a result, members of this kind of household not only feel unloved, they blame themselves for not being the kind of people who deserve to be loved. As a result the drive to earn love and acceptance through performance, pretending, and perfectionism always is there.

A One-Two Punch

Churches can be rigid and religious in much the same way as religious households are. Churches can perpetuate the lie that we must do good in order to be good.

Our churches are saturated with Christians from homes that are deeply religious. The problems you see in the church are exactly the same problems you see in the home and vice versa. Christians put on their very best performance every Sunday morning and attend churches where the pressure is to comply, conform, and "be on your best behavior."

In rigidly religious churches, church members may fail to "do what they are supposed to do" and experience the same kind of punishment, criticism, and rejection as they did in their own homes. The result always is tragic. The result always makes people believe they are under pressure to pretend. The result is the absence of real and genuine relationships.

Brennan Manning says in his book *The Ragamuffin Gospel*: "It may be that Christians, not withstanding corporate worship, common prayer, and all their fellowship in service, may still be left to their loneliness. The final breakthrough to fellowship does not occur because, though they have fellowship with one another as believers and as devout people, they do not have fellowship as the undevout, as sinners. The pious fellowship permits no one to be a sinner. So all must conceal their sins from themselves and from their fellowship. We dare not be sinners. Many Christians are unthinkably horrified when a real sinner is suddenly discovered among the righteous. So we remain alone with our sin, living in lies and hypocrisy. The fact is that we all are sinners" (pp. 130-131).

Sins, failures, mistakes, and shortcomings are not allowed if you go to church. If a Christian wants to be a part of a church, the only alternative is to pretend to be good while he or she hides shameful imperfections. As a result, many churches not only contribute to shame, they perpetuate it.

"Playing Church" Checklist

Are you attending a church that perpetuates pretending and hiding? Are you attending a church characterized by hypocrisy? If we can't find support, encouragement, and acceptance at church, then where in the world are we supposed to find it? At your church, do you feel valued? Do you experience a sense of belonging? Take out a pencil or pen. Read through the following characteristics of a shame-based, works-based, performance-based, religious church.

Place a check in the blanks that might describe your church:

1. _____ We all are saved; we all are good people.
2. _____ Our church has little diversity. Everyone basically looks alike, acts alike, thinks alike, and even dresses alike.
3. _____ We have it all together. We don't have any problems. We certainly don't share our problems with others. Sundays are days on which members put their best foot forward.
4. _____ Those who have problems are weak in their faith. They simply need to try more diligently and do better.
5. _____ Those who don't do what they are supposed to do, those who fail, those who don't measure up, and/or those who sin deserve to be punished.
6. _____ Any kind of emotions and enthusiasm are irreverent.
7. _____ No loving confrontation or church discipline exist. Gossip is rampant.
8. _____ If the lost need Christ, they know where the church is situated. That is why we pay the pastor.
9. _____ We are more like a religious social club than a fellowship dedicated to reaching the lost and ministering to the hurting.
10. _____ Members can be absent week after week and not be missed or contacted.
11. _____ Members believe that church is for them and what they can get out of it.

12. _____ A form of godliness exists but so does an absence of the power and presence of the Holy Spirit.
13. _____ Fewer than half of the members show up on any given Sunday.
14. _____ Most of those who attend do so for the worship service. Fewer go to Sunday school. Even fewer attend Sunday- and Wednesday-evening services.
15. _____ Most services follow the same basic format Sunday after Sunday.
16. _____ Baptisms are rare; testimonies from those who are miraculously saved are even more rare.
17. _____ The church has no strategy for mentoring, discipleship, and accountability relationships.
18. _____ The church has no strategy for ongoing evangelism. It has no strategy for prayer even though it has a multitude of programs and events.
19. _____A few of the members do the majority of the work of the church. They are overworked and overcommitted.
20. _____ The church places a huge focus on the pastor. He enjoys a "celebrity-like" status.

So, what do you think? How would you describe your church? Would you characterize your church as fake or faithful? What I have discovered in more than 20 years of ministry experience is that many people visit the church expecting something real, authentic, and genuine.

Tragically, they see many, if not most of the characteristics the checklist above identifies. They visit expecting to be loved, supported, encouraged, and accepted. They are dramatically disappointed when they discover that the members of the church are no different than are the people in the world—at times even worse.

On a personal note . . .

The church I attend is awesome. I have the freedom to be the person God made me to be and to find acceptance. The pastor of the church is the genuine article. My Sunday-school class is unbelievable. I don't know what my family and I would do without our church. Find a positive place in which you can find acceptance. Few things are worse than going to a church where tremendous pressure to be the perfect, problem-free Christian is found.

As a Christian counselor, every day I hear rigid and religious husbands say, "Fix my wife." Every day, I hear rigid and religious wives say, "Fix my husband." Rigid and religious parents say, "Fix my child." The message is, "Those who are closest to me—my loved ones—are unacceptable. They need to be fixed." The rigid and religious never realize and certainly never would admit that they are a big part, if not the biggest part, of the problem.

Before we move to the next section addressing how sexual sin contributes to our "playing at Christianity", take an opportunity to reflect on the atmosphere of your home and your church as you step into the spotlight in the following section.

You're in the Spotlight

We want our kids to do right and behave. We want our children to avoid doing wrong. We want our spouses to do what we say, make us happy, and meet our needs. We want our spouses to do what they are "supposed to do." Is having others do what you want them to do what is most important in your life? Is this so important that you yell, scream, lose your temper, explode in anger, threaten, harshly criticize, and withdraw love to get your way? Is your church a place at which you feel pressured to be perfect? Allow the

Lord to shed light into the areas of your life, your home, your upbringing, and your place of worship as you step into the spotlight.

1. Describe what growing up in your home was like. What characteristics from the "Hip Family Checklist" describe what your household was like when you were a child?

2. How did how you were reared impact you in a positive way as an adult? How did how you were reared impact you in a negative way in your closest relationships? How has your relationship with your parents influenced your relationship with Christ?

3. How does how you were parented influence how you parent your own children? For the better? For the worse?

4. How do your rigid rules and demand for compliance contribute to the shame of those in your household? How does your pretending to be someone you are not negatively impact those closest to you?

5. On a scale from 1 to 10 (1 being rigid and religious to 10 being real and accepting), what number would you select to describe your family? What number would you select to describe your church? Explain your answers.

Stepping into God's Light

Heavenly Father,

Forgive us for our hypocrisy. Forgive us for being one way at church and a much different way at home. Forgive us for acting one way with our fellow employees or boss and a much different way at home. You know that if we acted at church the way we act at home, we would be ex-communicated. If we acted in the workplace like we act at home, we would be fired that day. Forgive us for our demands for perfection when we are so far from it. Forgive us for always demanding our way and demanding to be served. Forgive us for the destruction and damage we have caused because of our own selfishness.

Heavenly Father, forgive us for our hypocrisy. We are so quick to judge, criticize, and gossip. Like riding on a see-saw, we push others down to lift ourselves up. Teach us to see others, love others, serve others, forgive others, and accept others as You would—beginning in our own homes and churches. Now lead us, guide us, and protect us as we look at sexual sin—the greatest reason for hiding, pretending, and shame that exists in our churches and homes today.

We pray in the Name of Jesus. Amen.

Chapter 4

Sex, Lies, and Videotape

It is God's will that you should be sanctified: that you should avoid sexual immorality, that each of you should learn to control his own body in a way that is holy and honorable (1 Thess. 4:3).

For God did not call us to be impure, but to live a holy life. Therefore, he who rejects this instruction does not reject man but God, who gives you his Holy Spirit (1 Thess. 4:7-8).

As we have seen so far, Christians have several reasons that they pretend. They pretend because of devastating and heartbreaking rejection from the past. As a result they believe they are unworthy of love. They pretend because they grow up in rigid and religious households. They pretend and perform and please in order to earn what they want the most—love, approval, and acceptance.

As we shall see in this chapter, Christians pretend in order to hide secret sins. I believe that sexual sin is the number-one contributor to shame in the hearts and lives of Christians today. I believe that sexual sin is the number-one reason for hypocrisy in the church today. I believe that sexual sin is the number-one sin that Christians hide today.

Whenever sexual sin exists, guilt and shame are conceived. Guilt and shame are the twin products of sexual sin. Whenever guilt and shame exist, hiding and pretending always do, also. Whenever hiding occurs, so do lies, dishonesty, and sneaking around.

Lights, Camera, Action!

A new character has entered the scene. She is longing and lonely. She is searching and anxious. She believes love is passing her by. She believes she is not deserving of love. She believes she is not worthy. She settles for anyone and anything. Getting what she wants and needs is up to her. She is cunning. She is clever. She doesn't give up easy. Her name is "Desperation." She would do anything for love.

Tasting the Forbidden Fruit

After trusting Jesus as Savior and Lord, Janet enjoyed four glorious months of walking with the Lord and knowing Him. She basked in the peace and fulfillment of total forgiveness. Beyond a doubt she knew she was saved. Beyond a doubt she knew that God existed. The change in her life was dramatic. For her, things were like day and night—until she allowed the darkness to set in once again.

At church she met a guy. He was absolutely beautiful. She wanted so much to be popular and loved. They went out a couple of times. The relationship did not seem to either of them to be very serious. One night he went to her house to talk. She lived in a very nice house in a very nice neighborhood. Her parents were home. He met them. They were great people. Her dad was a deacon in the church. Her mom was a Sunday-school teacher for preschoolers. Her parents said that they were going out to meet with friends from church that evening. Janet said she never will forget what her dad said before he left. He said, "We are leaving you two alone tonight because we trust you. We know that our daughter knows right from wrong and that she never would do anything that we would disapprove of while we are away. You two have a nice evening." Then he and her mom left.

The front door barely had shut behind her parents before Janet was leading her guest upstairs to her bedroom. She put on some soft music. She lowered the lights and began taking off all of her clothing. Needless to say, one thing led to another; they had sex together. She was scared. She had no idea what she was doing. She never had been with a guy before. She had the following to say:

"To be perfectly honest, it was a humiliating and horrible experience for me. It sure wasn't like you see in the movies. The joy I experienced in the Lord was gone immediately. I felt dirty. I felt so guilty and ashamed. The feelings of being unworthy, unlovable, and unforgivable became part of my life. For weeks I asked myself the same questions and made the same statements over and over:

"How could I have done such a horrible thing against God?

"How could I have betrayed Him?

"How could I have been so stupid?

"How could God ever forgive me?

"How could I ever forgive myself?

"I don't deserve to live.

"I wish I never had been born.

"I am so ashamed.

"No punishment was too great for me. I threw away everything that was good, wholesome, and pure and exchanged these great gifts for shame, regret, and dishonesty. I learned an important lesson that I never will forget: Whenever sexual sin is found, shame is there also."

Why would anyone ever share a story such as this and allow me to print it—even with the name changed? For her entire life she punished herself for her "fall from grace." She tried so desperately to make up for her past that she made herself and everyone around her miserable. "No more!" she yelled. She also said that she wanted to be the first church member to admit that she had sinned in her past. Her courage and honesty certainly inspired me.

The last line of her quote is what stood out to me the most. "Whenever sexual is found, shame is there also." I have heard some people say, "All sins are equal." I do not agree, in terms of the magnitude of impact that sexual sin has on the sinner. Sexual sin is different from other sins in that it impacts us at the core of who we are. It destroys us at the core of who we are. For a few moments of sexual gratification we sacrifice Christian character and Christian integrity. We feel dirty. We feel guilty. We feel ashamed. We hide. We live in a culture that is saturated by sex. Tragically we are part of a church in America that is saturated by sex as well. As a result, we have a shame-saturated culture and a shame-saturated church. Whenever you find shame, you always find hypocrisy.

Porn Again

I know what you are thinking. Why does this guy talk to the "born again" about "porn again?" First of all, I believe the problem of sexual sin and hiding sexual sin is a huge problem in our churches and in our homes. Second, I don't think the church is addressing the problem at all. Third, I have five daughters. Our sex-saturated culture and our sex-saturated homes scare me to death. I am afraid for the safety of my daughters. Maybe you think I'm overreacting or just being paranoid. Earlier I mentioned a few statistics. Take a closer look at the following statistics reported by Family Safe Media (*www.familysafemedia.com/pornography_statistics.html*). Maybe you will be motivated to fight this battle with me:

- Pornography generates 57 billion dollars every year worldwide.
- In America the revenue earned through pornography—approximately 12 billion dollars each year—is more than the professional football, baseball, and basketball franchises combined.
- In America the revenue earned through pornography is more than the major networks ABC, CBS, and NBC earn combined.
- The networks listed above, not including cable, broadcast 65,000 references to sexual behavior in one year.
- More than 100,000 websites offer illegal child pornography. Child pornography generates three billion dollars every year.
- More than 90 percent of 8- to 16-year-olds have viewed pornography online. Mostly they've viewed it while doing homework. More than 70 percent of all pornography falls into the hands of children. By junior high more than 90 percent of boys and more

than 70 percent of girls have viewed hard-core pornography.

• The average age of first Internet exposure to pornography is 11 years old for boys and 13 for girls. The largest consumers of Internet pornography range in age from 12-17.

• More than 40 percent of those struggling with sexual addiction are women.

• FBI statistics say your child has a 100-percent chance of meeting a predator in a chat room.

• More than 70 percent of young men have sex before marriage. Now for the first time more than 50 percent of young women have sex before marriage.

• More than 60 percent of all websites on the Internet are pornographic web sites.

• As of September 2000, children were spending 65-percent more of their time viewing pornographic sites than they were viewing game sites.

• More than 85 percent of kids surveyed said that their parents did not know what they viewed on the Internet.

• United States phone companies estimate that 70 percent of the 500,000 daily calls to "dial-a-porn" are made by minors.

• America has more than 20,000 outlets selling illegal, hard-core pornography—more locations than McDonalds.

• More than 60 percent of employees receive adult-oriented personal emails and view Internet sex sites at work.

• Playboy's web site, which offers free teaser shots of its Playmates, averages five million hits per day. Since the introduction of Playboy magazine 30 years ago, sexual violence against women has increased 500 percent.

• UNICEF estimates that one million children are forced into prostitution or used to produce pornography each year.

• The Department of Justice states that "Never before in the history of telecommunications media in the United States has so much indecent (and obscene) material been so easily accessible by so many minors in so many American homes with so few restrictions."

• Internet pornography now ranks highest of all causes of divorce.

To say the least, these statistics are alarming and heartbreaking. The last statistic, however, is what concerns me the most. Internet pornography now ranks as the highest of all causes of divorce. The church does not even address the problem. This is a huge secret. I'm also concerned that the statistics for pornography and sexual sin in the church are just as alarming and heartbreaking as they are for the world. According to research conducted by Patrick Means and reported in his book, *Men's Secret Wars* (pp. 132-133), he states that more than two-thirds of Christian men are involved in sexual sin in one form or another. According to Means, other independent Christian organizations such as *Christianity Today* and Promise Keepers confirm these alarming statistics. For example:

• According to a poll by Promise Keepers, close to 70 percent of Christian men and Christian leaders struggle with sexual sin.

• More than half of all committed laymen and pastors have had some kind of inappropriate involvement with a woman either emotional or physical outside of marriage.

• Close to 40 percent of pastors surveyed confessed to have been involved in inappropriate sexual behavior with someone in the church.

• More than half of all Promise Keeper men reported to have viewed pornography in the past week.

• More than 60 percent of married Christian men fantasize about being with women other than their wives.

• More than 60 percent of all married men masturbate weekly.

• More than 90 percent of men reared in Christian homes were exposed to pornography while they were growing up.

• Few, if any, Christian men reach out for help. Less than five percent of Christian leadership and laymen report to having a close friend or confidant.

This means that just about every man you meet in any church on any given Sunday is involved with or struggling with some kind of sexual sin. If sexual sin and pornography now are among the top reasons for divorce, no wonder our church families literally are falling apart at the seams. What is my prediction based on the data? As the family goes, so goes the country. Maybe you are not yet as determined as I am do something about this tremendous threat to the security of our homes. Maybe you are not so concerned. If not, take a look at the following consequences of sexual sin.

Killer Sex

It kills me. I don't think I can take it anymore. I don't think I can hear another Christian couple who are dating say, "We are not hurting anybody by having sex. We love each other." I don't think I can hear another Christian man or woman say, "I'm not hurting anybody by looking at pornography. Nothing's wrong with visiting chat rooms." As a counselor and professor I don't go through a day without hearing from someone trapped in sexual sin. Christians seem to believe, "Hey, I go to church every Sunday. I pay my taxes. I don't commit murder, or drink, or smoke. What's wrong with sexual sin?" Well, for one thing, sexual sin kills open, honest, intimate fellowship with Christ and others. If the destruction of your fellowship with Christ is not enough, countless other consequences for sexual sin exist. I dedicate this section to those Christians who believe that nothing is wrong with sexual sin.

The greatest cost of sexual sin is the loss of openness, honesty, and intimacy in our most cherished relationships with Christ and others. Ultimately, those trapped in sexual sin lose their integrity, lose their character, and are forced to dedicate their entire lives to pretending. Having fellowship with Christ and other Christians is impossible when sexual sin exists. Living a Spirit-filled life when you are trapped in sexual sin is impossible. Being obedient when you are trapped in sexual sin is impossible. Experiencing the abundant life that God intends when you are trapped in sexual sin is impossible. When you are trapped in sexual sin, becoming the person that God intends for you to be is impossible. When you are trapped in sexual sin, experiencing love, joy, peace, patience, goodness, gentleness, kindness, and self-control is impossible. Instead you experience loneliness, isolation, and misery. In essence, sexual sin locks Christians inside a living hell isolated from Christ and others. If these costs are not enough in and of themselves, many other costs to sexual sin are apparent.

Another huge cost of sexual sin is that your sin is passed on to future generations. While they grow up more than 90 percent of Christian young boys are exposed to pornography. The overwhelming majority of Christian young men are exposed to pornography for the first time through finding magazines their own dads hide in their own homes. Christian men look at pornography and always say, without fail, "I'm not hurting anybody else." Devastating consequences for sexual sin exist. This happens not only to those engaging in sexual sin but to everybody around them.

I believe that those graphic sexual images permanently are etched into the hearts, minds, and souls of the young children that discover the material. I cannot tell you how many stories I have heard from people who are destroyed by sexual sin. When I begin examining their sexual history, story after story after story begins with the young man or young woman discovering pornography in his or her own home. Even though we may be forgiven for our own, personal sexual sins, we still pass the consequences down to future generations. If you don't believe me, just read the story about King David.

Sexual sin always gives Satan a foothold for other sins and problems. Christians involved in sexual sin are discouraged, depressed, ashamed, negative, critical, judgmental, self-righteous, and live a lie. They are prone to outbursts of anger, rage, and suicide. Those involved in sexual sin have a tendency to overeat, overwork, overspend, and overindulge themselves. They lose respect for themselves and for others. They lose balance and live at the extremes. They live in blatant rebellion to God and His best. Sexual sin invades and slowly takes control of every area of life. When we are stressed out and anxious, under pressure or overwhelmed, we soothe ourselves through sexual gratification. When we want to escape and entertain ourselves—when we are bored, when we feel lonely, isolated, or want to reward ourselves, we look to gratify ourselves sexually. When we want to feel loved, we engage in sexual sin. As Christians our entire lives soon are dominated by sexual sin.

It becomes our master as life continues to spiral downward out of control. One morning we wake up and wonder how in the world we ever let things go so far.

Another cost of sexual sin is precious time. Recently, I turned 40. Now, more than any time in my entire life, I regret the wasted years spent living for myself and for my own needs and ambitions. Now, more than ever, my greatest desire is to surrender my whole being in living each moment for the glory of God. Nothing gives me greater satisfaction. For the Christian trapped in sexual sin, endless hours are spent on the Internet. Endless hours are spent hiding. Endless hours are spent sneaking around. Endless time, energy, and effort are spent living a lie. Endless hours are spent living in fear. Wasted time, wasted energy, wasted effort, and wasted resources never will be yours again.

Constant control is another consequence of sexual sin. Surrender to Christ as Lord is the key to the victorious Christian life. Those trapped in sexual sin do the opposite. Their desire is for control. A Christian cannot possibly completely control one area of life and live an obedient, open, honest, and surrendered life in every other area of life. Christians trapped in sexual sin learn that they can meet their own sexual needs or use others to meet those needs and keep their public lives and public images looking good. They learn to live independently of God. They work even more diligently to be successful in the world's eyes—even in God's eyes—but most importantly in their own eyes at the expense of being led, filled, and empowered by the Holy Spirit. As long sexual sin is a problem, the Holy Spirit always is quenched.

Another huge cost of sexual sin is that it distorts God's incredible and miraculous gift of sex. Sex is designed for marriage. Sex is a beautiful picture of how two become one. It is a beautiful picture of our relationship with Christ. With pornographic images etched into our minds and hearts, with sexual partners and experiences etched into our minds and hearts, sex with our spouses never will be as it was intended to be. Yes, forgiveness can occur, but sexual sin always has consequences. Besides, sexual sin is not fair for our spouses. At least 20 times a day my 5-year old son says, "It's not fair." Comparing or expecting our spouses to live up to the beautiful, well-endowed, sexual dynamos we dream and fantasize about is not fair. Just for your information, those people aren't real.

Another cost of sexual sin is that enough never is enough. Once we are trapped in sexual sin, we never can find enough on the Internet, or in magazines, or in movies to satisfy the depths of our depravity. We never can find enough partners to satisfy the depths or our sexual desires. The dangers of sexual sin on the Internet, in magazines, and/or chat rooms have the potential of leading to more dangerous and compromising situations. In other words, we deal not only with spiritual death but also with the potential for physical death through sexually transmitted diseases, suicide, sexual predators, and abortion. The Guttmacher Institute, a special affiliate of Planned Parenthood, reports that 44,670,812 abortions have been performed in the U.S. since Roe v. Wade in 1973 until 2003. That is one baby aborted every 24 seconds, 150 every hour, 3,597 every day, 25,250 babies every week, 109,416 babies every month, and counting (*www.mccl.org/abortion_statistics.htm*).

A final cost of sexual sin is that it distorts our view of sin in general. In other words, if we can rationalize sexual sin, we can rationalize any sin. What we forget when we are consumed and driven by our own selfish needs is that sin breaks the heart of God and quenches the power of the Holy Spirit. We can be successful. We can do great things for God. We can be respected by all of those around us and even by those who are closest to us. What we do not have is love, joy, peace, patience, kindness, goodness, gentleness, and self-control. What we do not have is the opportunity to share God's love with those around us. God cannot possibly channel His love, His power, His mercy, His forgiveness, and His goodness through those of us who are trapped in sexual sin. All accomplishments, achievements, and successes we perform in the Name of God in the midst of our sin are simply wood, hay, and straw.

Maybe you are thinking, "Well, I don't know. I still don't think my sexual sin hurts anybody." If so, give me a holler. You need professional help.

On a Personal Note . . .

I know I harp quite a bit on sexual sin in the church. I do have five daughters. I am afraid for them. I am afraid because of how men might look at my precious girls. Sexual sin portrayed through pornography, movies, magazines, and television distorts a biblical and godly view of sex. It distorts the way a man looks on a woman. It distorts the beautiful gift that God has provided. Perverted and disgusting images and scenes are permanently etched into our minds and hearts. Of course, once we see those things, we want to try them out. It's just how we are. I pray that a time of cleansing and repentance would begin in our homes and churches. If not, I pray for God's swift judgement beginning with His own people—beginning with me.

You're in the Spotlight

Living in a sex-saturated society and more than likely attending a church plagued by sexual sin makes experiencing and embracing a life of sexual purity almost impossible. "Everybody's doing it" seems to be the norm. Sexual purity and holiness are gifts from God. Maintaining sexual purity is a daily battle. How are you allowing God to win this battle in your life? Take a moment to get out a pen or pencil. Allow God's light to shine in your life, specifically in the area of sexual sin, as you reflect on the following questions:

1. What do you think about the statistics related to sexual sin in America? What do you think about the statistics regarding sexual sin in the church?

2. Review the consequences of sexual sin. Which of the consequences of sexual sin has been most devastating for you? How are you continuing to punish yourself for the sexual sins of your past?

3. We are forgiven for our sexual sins completely, but the consequences of those sins can last a lifetime. Do you agree or disagree? Explain your answer. What are some examples from the Bible?

4. Rate yourself. On a scale from one to 10 (one being habitual involvement in sexual sin to 10 being sexually pure and holy on a consistent basis), how do you rate yourself? Identify those areas of sexual sin that hinder you from enjoying the abundant life God intends you to have. Spend a time of confession, openness, and honesty before God.

5. Who is holding you accountable in the area of sexual purity? I believe maintaining a sexually pure life outside of open, honest, "tough-loving," accountability relationships is impossible. Do you agree or disagree? How did you arrive at this conclusion?

Stepping into God's Light

Heavenly Father,

Thank you for the privilege of praying to you as we travel in this journey together. We humble ourselves before You and recognize You as Lord. In this attitude of humility we seek your forgiveness for our greatest hypocrisy of all—our involvement in sexual sin. We pretend the problem doesn't exist. We certainly pretend that the problem does not exist with us.

Forgive us for our hypocrisy. Forgive us for daily putting before our eyes those things that dishonor You on television, in movies, on the Internet, and other forms of media. Give us the grace to be honest and clean before You and others. Help us to live lives of holiness and purity. Help us to support, encourage, and hold each other accountable in this raging battle. Father, give us the grace to turn from our wicked ways.

You promise:

"If my people, who are called by my name, will humble themselves and pray and seek my face and turn from their wicked ways, then I will hear from heaven and will forgive their sin and will heal their land" (2 Chron. 7:14).

Father, we desperately need your healing and holiness. Help us to realize that sexual sin costs us everything that is most beautiful in life—our Christian character and integrity and open, honest, genuine relationships with You and others. Help us to realize that when we sacrifice these things, we sacrifice everything. Now, heavenly Father, go with us while we address resentment, or our unwillingness to forgive—yet another huge contributor to our hiding and pretending.

We pray in the Name of Jesus. Amen.

Chapter 5

Best Supporting Actor

For I see that you are full of bitterness and captive to sin (Acts 8:23).

See to it that no one misses the grace of God and that no bitter root grows up to cause trouble and defile many (Heb. 12:15).

Be kind and compassionate to one another, forgiving each other, just as in Christ God forgave you (Eph. 4:32).

So far, in our journey together, we have examined why we hide and why we pretend. We hide and pretend because deep down in our hearts reside fear, insecurity, inadequacy, and deep feelings of shame. We hide the pain and rejection from our past. We hide our feelings of insecurity and inadequacy because good enough was never good enough. We hide all the things we do to try and make ourselves feel better. In other words we hide and pretend to protect our secret sins. In this chapter we will examine yet another huge contributor to our hiding and pretending—resentment, or our unwillingness to forgive. As Christians we hide our hate and desire to punish when we are wronged. It's called "passive aggression." If shame is the star of the show, then resentment definitely is the best supporting actor.

Lights, Camera, Action!

A new character enters the scene. He lies just beneath the surface. Any frustration can set him off. He is dangerous and volatile. Sometimes, he absolutely is out of control. He is poison and slow death. He spews his venom in the most cutting and critical ways. At the same time he is a powerful motivator. He is fuel to propel and excel its possessor beyond all others. He is the number-one destroyer of open, honest, and intimate relationships with Christ and with others. His name is Resentment.

Addicted to Hate

I met her while I worked at a secular counseling center at a major university. She was beautiful, tall, slender, and African-American. Everyone knew her. She literally was "Miss Everything" on campus—homecoming queen, academic athlete of the year, and vice-president of her class. She desperately needed help. Before long the beauty of her image began to crack from within. She said she no longer wanted to live. I examined the seriousness of her threat. She thought about suicide every day but assured me she never would follow through.

The more we talked, the more I realized the root cause of her despair centered on a father who never expressed love or approval. No matter how diligently she tried, what she did never was good enough. Good enough never was good enough for him.

The last time she saw her father was five years earlier at his funeral. I told her if she wanted to move forward, she must let go of the hatred she harbored in her heart toward her father. I never will forget what she said and how she said it. She said, "I can't let go of my hate. My hate keeps me going. My hate is why I succeed. I must hang onto my hate." What I saw in her face was deep despair and unbelievable determination. After that day I never saw her again.

The unwillingness to forgive is at the heart of resentment. Resentment can be defined as the unwillingness to forgive and determination to hold on to our right to punish. At least that's how I define it. Whenever we bury our anger and hurt, we bury them alive. Ultimately, they consume and control us. The result of harboring bitterness and resentment in our hearts is the slow and certain death of our souls. Resentment kills emotional and spiritual growth. Resentment not only kills us, it kills those around us as well. We lash out in hate. Cut us off in traffic, and see what you get. Resentment always kills open, honest, and intimate relationships with Christ and with others. When you find resentment, you always find blame, punishment, and the harsh control of others—especially those who are closest to us. At the same time, on the surface, in the public eye, for those we are striving to please, we are beautiful to behold.

The Benefits of Bitterness

If resentment is so devastating to our lives, hearts, and souls, then why in the world would anyone in his or her right mind hold on to resentment and bitterness? Now, this is a great question. Of course, the answer must be that resentment serves some kind of purpose or that some kind of benefit is derived from holding on to our hate and hurts from the past. What are those benefits? I'm glad you asked. Holding on to resentment and bitterness has at least four important benefits.

First of all, holding on to resentment feels powerful. Few things feel more powerful than holding on to hate. With great satisfaction we tell ourselves that we have every right to hate. We have every right to retaliate. We have every right to withdraw, criticize, yell, scream, punish, and demand that the other person do whatever is required to get back in our good graces. Now, doesn't that sound absolutely fantastic? It sure feels good at the time. It sure feels powerful at the time—to hang something over someone else's head, especially over a loved one's head. We want that person to hurt just as we have been hurt. We hang on to resentment, hate, and bitterness because it feels powerful.

Another reason for hanging on to resentment is that hate and hurt from the past can serve as powerful motivators to push us to excel beyond all others. Hate becomes the fuel that drives your inner need to succeed and to prove that you are somebody. Each success provides the opportunity for us to say to our past accusers and critics, "Hey, you were wrong about me!"

My favorite example of how hate can motivate is in the movie *Waterboy* with Adam Sandler. In the show Adam Sandler is the waterboy for a struggling and desperate college football team. One day one of the football players on the team was picking on him. This football player was making fun of the Waterboy because he was "a bit slow." Or, how his mom described him, "He doesn't have watch you call, de social skills." Out of anger, the Waterboy tackles this player. He actually knocks him out. He crushes him.

As a result, the coach invites the Waterboy to become a part of the team. During the first practice, the coach, played by Henry Winkler, invites the Waterboy to show the entire team his ability to tackle. The Waterboy fails miserably. The coach asks, "Where is your intensity? How were you able to make such a beautiful tackle the other day?" Adam Sandler replied, "I just thought about all of the people in my past who hurt me." The coach replied, "That's it. Think of all the people who have hurt you in the past. Visualize and attack. We will call it your 'tackling fuel'." The Waterboy visualized all the people who hurt him in the past. He became the leading tackler and led his team to victory. No doubt about it—hate can motivate. We hang on to resentment, hate, and bitterness because these very emotions can motivate us to excel beyond all others.

Besides power and performance, another huge benefit for holding on to resentment is protection. Resentment, hate, and bitterness can form a protective wall around our hearts to keep us from getting hurt. We actually resolve in our hearts, "I never will be hurt again!" With hate and hurt we can hide our heart from pain and the risk of rejection while we put up a good front—sometimes even a great front. We can appear to be the dedicated, devoted, sacrificial Christian while we stay safe. It's a great combination. I believe that **outside of sexual sin, resentment, or the unwillingness to forgive, is the greatest contributor to hypocrisy in the church.**

Power, performance, and protection sound like some great benefits to me. But, I see one more, pretty nice perk. Pity is another great benefit to holding onto resentment. We hold onto our hate and hurts from the past while we cry out, "Life's not fair!" We also yell out to God and others statements such as, "How could you let this happen to me? I thought you loved me." We then have every right to get the pity party started. We begin sending out invitations to our pity party. We invite our best pity-party friends. We put on our best pity-party clothes. We play our favorite pity-party songs. We get our favorite pity-party gifts—attention, sympathy, and the right to give up and quit. We give ourselves permission to stay mad at God and any and everyone else who ever has let us down. So, with all of these great benefits, the big question then becomes, "Why in the world would we ever let go of our resentment and bitterness?" You ask some of the best questions.

The Ravages of Resentment

Unfortunately, for much of my Christian life, I enjoyed the benefits of resentment and bitterness. At the same time, the benefits of bitterness are enjoyed at an extremely high price.

As the Lord held up the mirror reflecting my Christian life, I saw at least five devastating results for hanging on to resentment, bitterness, hate, and hurt from the past. We have looked at several benefits of resentment. Let's take an opportunity to look at some of the costs. Then, you can determine for yourselves if you want to continue to hang on to all of your past hate and hurt. I just want you to be able to make an informed choice.

One of the most devastating consequences of holding on to our resentment, or our unwillingness to forgive, is that love and light are blocked. Resentment is what I call a "Son Blocker." Resentful Christians can't possibly remain in fellowship with Christ. God's love and light are what make growing and maturing as Christians possible. This is exactly why literally thousands of church members who have been Christians for 10, 20, or 30 years still have the spiritual and emotional maturity of 12-year olds or 16-year olds. Emotional and spiritual growth die the moment resentment is born. Resentment is born the exact moment we make the decision, "I will not forgive." Christians who are unwilling to forgive can grow financially, intellectually, and physically. They may grow in their ability to work the system and please people, but emotionally and spiritually they remain unchanged—zero growth. In their capacity to give and receive love, they remain incapable. In their capacity to forgive and receive forgiveness, they remain unable. As a result, hate-filled, bitter Christians are competent, hard-working, sacrificial, successful, dependable, and deeply religious people. At the same time, close, personal, honest, growing, transparent relationships with Christ and others simply are non-existent.

A second devastating effect of holding on to bitterness and hate is what I call the "irony of resentment." The irony of resentment occurs when resentful Christians—those who are unwilling to forgive—begin to take on the same characteristics as the person or persons they hate the most. As a result, they begin to hurt the ones closest to them in the same way they were hurt. This ensures that resentment, hatred, and bitterness are passed on to future generations beginning with those closest to them—beginning with those who love them the most. Misery always loves company.

If these two devastating consequences are not enough, a third damaging impact of resentment is yet another "ironic twist." The ironic twist is that, over time, we begin to resent the very ones we are striving so hard to please. We perform. We pretend. We put on a show. We please in order to get what we want and then begin to hate the ones that give it to us. I know it sounds crazy. Why? First of all, only Christ and Christ alone can completely satisfy our deepest and innermost needs and desires. So, if we are looking to anyone except Christ to meet our needs, we always will be disappointed. Second, when we strive to please others through meeting their endless expectations, we are valued for what we do—never for who we are. We all know this deep down. We can dedicate our lives to a person, a group, an organization, or a company. These can turn on us in a second. The truth is no person or organization or ministry can give us what we truly need. As good as the praise, prestige, position, and power may be, only Christ and Christ alone can satisfy our deepest needs.

A fourth devastating impact of choosing to hold on to resentment, hate, and bitterness is what I call "the negative filter." Those we hate now or have hated in our past probably deserve it. They are jerks or worse. I will let you use your own adjectives. They deserve to be punished. After all, they hurt us deeply. We trusted them. But for just a moment consider with me this possibility. Those same people may have done all they could to love us and do what was in our best interest. The love they showed us might have far outweighed the hurt and the offenses. The tragedy is that when we choose to hang on to resentment and bitterness, we can't possibly see anything good. When we choose not to forgive, all we are able to see is the negative. We fail to see the good in others. We fail to see the beauty in the world. We fail to soak in, accept, and embrace the goodness of God. Also, because of resentment, we constantly look at the negative aspects of ourselves and thus contribute to a life of shame. Resentment is a huge contributor to shame. Whenever you find shame, you also find hypocrisy.

As a result, behind all of our goodness at church—behind closed doors—we are harsh, judgmental, whiners, gripers, and complainers. We do not appreciate all we have. Instead, we gripe about all of the things we don't have. The truth is that the world is imperfect. People are imperfect. This means that those we love and trust at some point will hurt us and let us down. Tragically we can allow imperfect people in an imperfect world to imprison us in misery, hate, disappointment, and resentment. Trust me. This prison is much worse than is any prison built by human hands.

A fifth and final devastating consequence of choosing not to forgive and to hang on to our bitterness and hate is loneliness and isolation—the absence of close, open, and honest relationships. This may be the most devastating consequence of all. We may be successful in the church and in the world. We may have power, prestige, respect, and many, many acquaintances. We may have fame and the very best the world and the church have to offer. But, hold on to resentment, bitterness, and hate, and then we are among the loneliest and most miserable people on earth. Resentment has the power to make us and keep us miserable. Show me a person who is unwilling to forgive; I will show you a failure at Christ-honoring relationships. Not only are we among the most miserable people on earth, we make everyone around us just as miserable and just as hateful. Those who are resentful pass their hate and their misery on to others, especially those who are closest to them. This is the legacy we leave.

> ***On a Personal Note . . .***
>
> *I have the most loving parents, in-laws, and spouse that anyone ever could have. I also happen to be on the overly sensitive side. What this means is that I have blown some really petty things way out of proportion, on occasion. As a result, I allowed bitterness to rob me of some precious time that I never, ever will get back. Resentment is a killer of the mind, heart, body, and soul. Resentment is a killer of love and relationships. Resentment hardens the heart. Resentment is a killer of everything good and beautiful in others and in the world. I had but one option—not only to beg for God's forgiveness but also to beg for the forgiveness of my loved ones as well. My mom, dad, wife, her parents, and my kids have my deepest and most heartfelt apology. Thanks for never giving up on me.*

The Raw Deal of Regret

I don't want to leave the topic of resentment without addressing regret. If resentment is our unwillingness to forgive others, regret is our unwillingness to forgive ourselves. When we are unwilling to forgive ourselves, we become our own worst enemy. We become our own worst critic. We punish ourselves, criticize ourselves, and kick ourselves to motivate ourselves to excel beyond all others. You'll find no more miserable person on earth than a Christian striving to make up for the sins from yesterday. Those who are the least forgiving of themselves are the least forgiving of others. Those of us who are the most critical of ourselves are the most critical of others. Show me a negative, judgmental, and critical Christian; I'll show you a Christian imprisoned by hate and hurt from his or her past. I actually know some Christians who believe their gift of "criticism" is a help or benefit to others. The bottom line is this: Regret-filled Christians cannot share the gift of God's forgiveness with others because they do not embrace the gift of God's forgiveness for themselves. They cannot possibly give away what they do not have.

When I think about "regret", the first thing that springs to mind is the television show "Hee Haw." As I grew up, I was forced to watch "Hee Haw." I still have not recovered mentally, emotionally, or psychologically. Every Saturday night, my family gathered to watch this show. I remember the "Hee Haw" cast getting together and singing about their heartbreaking woes. In the chorus, they would sing, "Gloom, despair, and agony on me. Deep, dark, depression, excessive misery. If it weren't for bad luck, I'd have no luck at all. Gloom, despair, and agony on me." For some reason when I think of the word "regret", I always think of this song.

Regret has everything to do with gloom, despair, and agony. In essence, regret simply is refusing to trust that God is "faithful and just and will forgive us our sins and purify us from all unrighteousness" (1 John 1:9). Why would a Christian refuse God's forgiveness? Great question. The answer is pride. The last thing a person hanging on to failures, sins, mistakes, and regrets will do is to admit that he or she is wrong. Regretful Christians will say, "But, you don't know what I've done. I don't deserve to be forgiven. I deserve to be punished. I did bad. I am bad. I deserve to be punished." Instead Christians plagued by regret vow to do better and try even harder. Regret becomes the fuel that drives the desire not only to do better but also to be the best, or even perfect in the case of neurotic Christians. Sins, mistakes, and failures of the past provide the motivation to excel, succeed, and rise above hurts and pains from the past. The great things regret-filled Christians do for God are not out of obedience but out of an attempt to make up for past sins.

The favorite phrase of regret-filled Christians is "if only." If only I were taller, or better looking, or smarter. If only I had a different job, or promotion, or better spouse, or bigger house, or nicer car. If only I had not made that decision in the past, my life would be so much better. If only I had what she has or what he has. The tragic result of hanging on to our disappointments from the past is that we start believing that life is not fair. Once we begin to believe that life is not fair, we begin to believe that God is not fair. Once we believe that God is not fair, we say in our minds and hearts, "Hey, God, look at all that I do for you. What are you doing for me?" We become angry. Once we become angry, we take control. Once we take control, Christ no longer is Lord. As a result, we rebel, turn our backs on Him, and invest our time, energy, and efforts in meeting our own selfish needs. The beautiful thing about hypocrisy is that we can appear to be the devoted, sacrificial, dedicated Christians in public while meeting our own personal needs behind the scenes. We can have the best of both worlds!

At least, the surface appears that way. Regret always leads Christians down the road to despair. Regretful Christians are not only disappointed with themselves, they also are disappointed with God. As a result, they trust in their own efforts and abilities to make up for yesterday's mistakes. **Making up for yesterday by being our best tomorrow always robs us of the joy we can experience today**.

Regret-filled Christians, holding on to the failures of the past, cannot ever experience joy, peace, contentment, or love. They are driven. They are productive. They definitely are religious. They pride themselves on doing everything they are supposed to do in just the right way. They are sacrificial and hard-working, but they also are incredibly difficult to love. It's like loving a porcupine. The closer you try and get to them, the more it hurts. On the surface they appear to be happy, successful, and devoted, but in reality, they are just pretending.

You're in the Spotlight

Once again, take time to allow God's truth to shine in some hidden places of your personal life. Before you move to the next section, take a moment to allow God's light and Spirit to guide you as you examine the following questions.

1. Pride can be described as our desperate attempt to be in control and to take care of things in our own strength—including our hurts and mistakes from the past. How is pride keeping you from forgiving others? How is pride keeping you from accepting God's forgiveness?

2. In this chapter resentment was described as the unwillingness to forgive and let go of your right to punish. How are you hanging on to resentment? Who are those people you simply are unwilling to forgive?

3. Four deadly results were identified for hanging on to resentment. Below list those devastating consequences below:

a.
b
c.
d.

Which one is doing the most damage in your life?

4. Whereas resentment was defined as the unwillingness to forgive others, regret was described as the unwillingness to forgive yourself. In what ways are you directing anger, hatred, and blame toward yourself?

5. Read 1 John 1:9. List all of things from your past that God will not forgive.

Stepping into God's Light

Heavenly Father,

You command us to forgive others as You forgive us (Eph. 4:32). You tell us if we do not forgive, You will not forgive us (Matt. 6:15). No matter who is at fault, You command us to reconcile with those who have something against us before we step foot in the worship service (Matt. 5:23). At the same time we are so unwilling to forgive. Whenever anyone does anything against us, we make sure they pay a price. We make them suffer. We hang on to our hate and hurt from the past and pretend that everything is OK. Forgive us, Father, for our unwillingness to forgive, especially when You have forgiven us totally and completely.

Lord Jesus, I don't know what's more tragic—our harsh, judgmental treatment of others or our harsh, judgmental treatment of ourselves. We can be our own worst enemy. We can be our own worst critic and punish ourselves without mercy. By your grace, Heavenly Father, allow us to see ourselves through your eyes. Give us the ability, by your grace, to embrace your love and your forgiveness in order for us to give these as your gifts to others. Help us to lighten up a bit—lighten our load by letting some things go. Heavenly Father, thank You for going with us as we look at the last reason for so much hiding and pretending that exists in the church.

We pray in Jesus' Name. Amen.

Chapter 6

A Brief Intermission

For God so loved the world that he gave his one and only Son, that whoever believes in him shall not perish but have eternal life (John 3:16).

That if you confess with your mouth, "Jesus is Lord", and believe in your heart that God raised him from the dead, you will be saved. For it is with your heart that you believe and are justified, and it is with your mouth that you confess and are saved (Rom. 10: 9-10).

Not everyone who says to me, "Lord, Lord", will enter the kingdom of heaven, but only he who does the will of my Father who is in heaven. Many will say to me on that day, "Lord, Lord, did we not prophesy in your name, and in your name drive out demons and perform many miracles?" Then I will tell them plainly, "I never knew you. Away from me, you evildoers!" (Matt. 7:21-23).

Let's take a break. Let's take an opportunity to see where we are and where we will go in these remaining chapters.

In the past chapters we looked at some of the reasons why we pretend. First of all, we pretend to hide our deep hurts and pain from the past. Second, we hide and pretend because of our feelings of failure stemming from how we were reared. We never really measured up. Good enough never was good enough. Third, we hide and pretend because of secret sins. We simply want to meet our own needs, in our own timing, in our own way. Fourth, we hide and pretend because of our unwillingness to forgive others and our unwillingness to forgive ourselves. We simply will not forgive, wipe the slate clean, and let go of our "right" to punish.

In this next chapter, we will look at one last reason for so much hiding and pretending and game-playing with people in the church. Many people in the church think they are saved, but they never have had a genuine salvation experience. They simply go through the motions.

Good News and Bad News

In this brief intermission before the show actually begins, I want to share some good news and some bad news. I'll share the bad news first. According to George Barna (*www.Barna.org*) more than 40 percent of church members in mainline Protestant denominations are not saved. What about the Good News? The Good News is that Christ died for you. He died to pay the price for your sin and rebellion. On the third day He rose from the grave. He is alive. He conquered sin and death. If you turn from living for yourself and place your faith and trust in Christ as Lord, you will be saved. Scripture says, "For it is by grace you have been saved, through faith—and this not from yourselves, it is the gift of God—not by works, so that no one can boast" (Eph. 2:8-9). You can do nothing to earn salvation. It is a gift of God. As with any gift, however, it can be accepted or rejected.

I'll never forget the day that Christ saved me. I was 16 years old. I grew up wild. I was very wild. "How wild were you?" I hear you asking. I was so wild that when I attended my 10-year high-school reunion, person after person remarked, "Wow, Steve, I can't believe you're still alive." One day when my family was away, I got a brand-new, Pink Floyd tape, "Dark Side of the Moon." I decided I would listen to my tape out in my car. I got in my car and popped the tape in the stereo. I thought I turned the key so that only the stereo would play. Without knowing I inadvertently started the engine. I may have hit my head on the steering wheel and regained consciousness. Somehow I managed to get out of the car and open the garage door to let out the toxic fumes. That moment was the closest I ever had been to death. For my family to have found me dead would have been tragic. They would have thought that I committed suicide when I was just listening to a new tape in my car. The whole event scared me.

That next Friday night I was at a Catholic church dance. I played football. On Friday nights after the games, the Prince of Peace Catholic Church sponsored a dance. I remember that the Rolling Stones were playing "I Can't Get No Satisfaction." At that particular moment God flashed my life before my eyes in an instant. I remember thinking and praying, "Lord, I am so sick of my life and of living for myself." Then I remember my prayer, "Lord, if you are up there, I am tired of living my life for myself. You must have a better way. Save me and forgive me. I no longer want to live for myself. I want to live for you. Amen."

After I prayed, I left the dance. Nothing seemed any different until I awoke the following morning. I believed that a big burden had been lifted from my shoulders. In the Person of Jesus Christ I discovered everything for which I had been searching. I had a hunger and thirst for God's Word. That day I began reading my Bible. I got rid of all my tapes and albums and anything from my past life. Sunday morning my dad got all of us together to go to church as a family. Through the amazing ministry of Damon Shook, Wally Cobb, and Champion Forest Baptist Church in Spring, TX, I began to understand the life-changing decision I made.

The Dark Side

I hear you saying, "So, Steve, what happened? You say you accepted Christ as Savior and Lord of your life. You also say that in the next chapter, 'the show' begins. This doesn't make any sense." After Jesus saved me in a miraculous way, life truly was amazing. Things were like night and day for me. If you can believe it, I continued to sin, make mistakes, and fail. I still had problems—even big problems at time. I was devastated every time I sinned against the God who saved me. I vowed to do better. I vowed to try more diligently. Except that the more diligently I tried, the more I failed until I began to experience "the dark side" of living the Christian life and the truth that just because we are saved doesn't mean we stop sinning. For me, as a new Christian, it was devastating.

I'm a huge *Star Wars* fan. I couldn't wait for *Star Wars III: Revenge of the Sith*. I parked so far away from the theater and waited in lines for so long that by the time I settled in my seat with a huge soda and a jumbo tub of popcorn, I had mountainous blisters all over my feet. The outcome was worth everything I put into it. The movie was everything I expected and more. The special effects, the creativity, and 20 years of loose ends finally being tied together fascinated me.

By far, the most captivating aspect of the show for me was observing Anakin Skywalker—young, talented, optimistic, and ambitious, with a huge desire to prove. Haunted by the pain of his past, combined with his insatiable desire for power, fueled by feelings of anger and fear, Anakin turned to the dark side. All the while, he justified his pursuit of power and praise by somehow thinking that love motivated his choices. The movie ends with Anakin standing beside the most powerful "man" in the universe—alone, burned, and devastated.

Haunted by the pain of my past, fueled by feelings of fear and anger, combined with a huge desire to prove to God and everybody else that I was worthy of love, I vowed to be the best Christian I could be. I justified climbing the "Christian ladder of success" by thinking that love motivated my accomplishments and achievements. The moment I took control—the moment I began living the Christian life *my* way for *my* glory—was the moment the pretending began. It continued for the next 17 years of my Christian life.

You're in the Spotlight

I bought into a devastating lie. The truth is no matter how diligently we try, no matter how good our intentions, we cannot live the Christian life in our own strength. Our greatest hope is to surrender our all to Christ each day and to allow Him to live His life through us by the ongoing filling of His Holy Spirit. For 17 years the more diligently I tried to be "good" and to do "good", the more miserable I became and the more miserably I failed.

As you step into the spotlight, take an opportunity to reflect on your personal salvation experience. If you do not have a personal relationship with Christ through a genuine salvation experience, talk to your pastor and/or fellow church member about your desire to learn more about getting this most important issue settled in your life.

1. Describe the day you trusted Christ as Savior and Lord of your life. When was it? Where was it? Who were the people involved? How did the Lord draw you into Himself?

2. Describe what your life was like before Christ and after Christ. How do you know you are genuinely saved?

3. What happened? What caused you to take back control? As a Christian what caused you to turn your back on God?

Stepping into God's Light

Heavenly Father,

Thank you for saving us. We are reminded of the price that Jesus paid on the cross for our sins. We are reminded of the movie, *Passion of the Christ.* Jesus died such a horrible and humiliating death to pay the price for our sin and rebellion. Thank you for loving us so much. Thank you for that reminder—in this brief intermission. Just like we couldn't save ourselves through our own efforts, we cannot live out the Christian life through our own efforts. We must depend on You. We must humble ourselves before You. We can do nothing without You. Forgive us, Father, for striving to do it all in our own strength for our own glory for so long.

Lord, please go with us as we move into these next chapters. I hate even to begin the next chapter. It's a painful reminder of my own efforts to live out the Christian life in my own strength. Forgive me for my stubbornness and pride. Forgive me for my desperate attempts to be "good enough" in Your eyes. Remind us, in these next chapters, that your love is not based on what we do or don't do, or on whether we succeed or fail. Your love for us is based on who You are. Who You are never changes. Open our hearts to this timeless truth.

We pray in the Name of Jesus. Amen.

Chapter 7

It's Show Time!

What good is it for a man to gain the whole world, yet forfeit his soul? (Mark 8:36).

The time finally has arrived for the show. Sit back and relax. Get the popcorn ready. Motivated by self-hatred, self-determination, past hurts, past mistakes, and resentment, I would prove to everyone—especially to God—that I was worthy of love. I was deeply hurt. I was desperate to be loved. In fact, I would have done anything to be loved and accepted. But a person only can be hurt so much before hurt turns to hate. Motivated by past hate and hurt, I would be the best I could be. I would prove to the ones who hurt me that they were wrong about me. I would be the best. I would be a success—no matter what the cost.

As a result I became all things to all people. My desire was to please, to fit in, and to belong. My greatest desires were to please and to prove. However, in the end, I pleased no one and proved nothing. I was trapped in an endless cycle of constantly being driven and continually being disappointed.

Failure was unacceptable. Giving up was not an option. I pushed myself even more. Past mistakes, sins, and failures combined with current mistakes, sins, and failures fueled my determination. I pushed myself. I punished myself. I kicked myself. I condemned myself and finally rose to my feet more determined than ever to try even more diligently.

As with any actor the overwhelming desire was for applause, approval, and recognition. I became a modern-day hypocrite. The applause and praise of people temporarily soothed like a drug all my past hurt and pain. I hid. I played a role. Behind "picture-perfect performance" I hid my feelings of shame, inadequacy, and fear.

Tragically in the midst of the applause, I began to experience success—something I never had experienced before. It became a cheap substitute for what I really needed.

Lights, Camera, Action!

"Sweet Success" entered the scene. She made her appearance on stage; the crowd went wild! The audience members stood to their feet. Over and over they shouted, "Encore. Encore. Encore!" Success was beautiful to behold. Success was like a drug. Success was intoxicating. Success was impressive. Success was addicting. Enough never was enough. The taste of success was sweet. I couldn't get enough.

The Making of a Religious Leader

Success fuels our pretending and performing. Success is what we crave. Success is the key to what we desire most—love, acceptance, approval, praise, power, and position. Success is based on our best performance. "What's wrong with success?" I hear you asking. Success is where Christianity and the world merge. Tragically, in the sick society in which we live, both Christians and non-Christians desperately desire success. Success has everything to do with our skills, talents, performance, and ability to work the system. Success has nothing to do with obedience. Obedience results from a daily, intimate, radical trust in Christ that oftentimes leads to suffering, rejection, misunderstanding, criticism, and what might appear as failure according to our society's standards. Success has nothing to do with obedience.

Success is the drive to be the very best in every area of life. As a result we feel good about ourselves. As a result we believe we are good people. Obedience says, "No matter how much I try, I cannot be good. My only hope is found in the daily, step-by-step, abiding trust and submission to Christ as Lord." Obedience has nothing to do with success and the drive to impress. Obedience has everything to do with trust and with the daily surrender of control. Unfortunately what is required to be a successful religious leader is success. The secret of ambition of "Make-Believers" is to climb the ladder of success, whether they do it in the church or in the world. **Success and the drive to impress comprise the difference between the phony and the faithful.**

Speaking of being phony I'd prefer to hide these next two chapters from you. I'd rather not talk about my own personal pretending and performing. Instead I'd rather talk about a fellow church member, or a "friend" on the mission field, or my neighbor down the street. Instead I am choosing not to hide and to share with you my own heartbreaking involvement with hypocrisy. Did I mention how difficult emerging from hiding is?

In striving to prove that I was somebody—in dedicating my life to earning love, approval, and acceptance—I just became dirtier and dirtier, more self-centered, more discouraged, and more ashamed. Every failure and every mistake became more motivation to try even more diligently. I was trapped. As a result living my Christian life became a "me" thing:

My best,
My performance,
My contentment,
My comfort,
My mistakes,
My failures,
My victories,
My successes,
My fears,
My past,
My future,
My image,
My needs,
My wants,
My desires,

My dreams,
My happiness,
My disappointments,
My agenda,
My ideas,
My plans,
My rights.

My service, my diligent work, my dedication, my accomplishments, and my successes ultimately were for my personal gain.

I began working out. I took karate. After my junior-high days I vowed that no one ever would hurt me physically again. I graduated from college with a 2.5 grade-point average in psychology. I was ready to call the "Psychiatric Hotline." You've never dialed this hotline? It goes something like this:

> Welcome to the Psychiatric Hotline.
> If you are obsessive-compulsive, please press 1 repeatedly.
> If you are co-dependent, please ask someone to press 2.
> If you have multiple personalities, please press 3, 4, 5, and 6.
> If you are paranoid-delusional, we know what you want. Just stay on the line so we can trace the call.
> If you are schizophrenic, listen carefully. A little voice will tell you which number to press.
> If you are depressed, which number you press doesn't matter. No one will answer.
> If you are delusional and occasionally hallucinate, please be aware that the thing you are holding on the side of your head is alive and is about to bite off your ear.

So what is a person supposed to do with a degree in psychology and no job experience? Where does a person go with a terrible GPA, no job skills, no direction, and with something to prove to God and to others? That's right. I enrolled in a Baptist theological seminary. After a ton of paperwork, some good references, and an interview, I was in. Surely God would be impressed with a 92-hour degree in theology.

I moved to Fort Worth, TX, from College Station with $400 of graduation money from college, a Pioneer stereo, and my clothes. And I thought Victoria, TX, was bad. From the first day on the seminary campus, I never felt as though I really "fit in" with the Baptist crowd, especially in the seminary dorm where I lived. Yeah, I was living in the seminary dorm—yet another shameful moment in my life. My perception of the dorm was that God picked up the United States and shook it. The weirdest people ended up at seminary. God then picked up the seminary and shook it. All the weirdest seminary students ended up in the dorm. And there I was, wondering how in the world I got there.

Never Say Never

Three years later "she" entered my life. "She" was waiting for class to begin in my "Introductory to the Baptist Hymnal" class. In my opinion learning about the Baptist hymnal was going to be about as much fun as a root canal. But things were looking better.

At this time in my life, I had a fairly long, "I-Will-Never-Ever-Again-Date-This-Kind-of-Person" list. I vowed that I never would get involved with a girl who—

- was a Baptist;
- ever went to my high school;
- ever was a cheerleader or on the drill team;
- ever attended Baylor University, or especially
- any girl who, for any reason, ever stepped foot on a Baptist seminary campus.

In each of these categories I had a nightmarish history with girls. I promised with all of my heart, mind, soul, and strength that I never would get involved with another girl who fit into any of these categories. Unbeknownst to me, I soon would learn another important lesson about "never saying never."

Then, I saw Karen for the first time. I remember walking into my class with my shiny, new Baptist Hymnal and seeing her for what I thought was the first time. I stood still in my tracks. I continued to look at her. I remember Karen was writing something on a notepad. She looked up for approximately one-and-a-half seconds and then began writing again. I still was frozen. I remained frozen for what seemed like an eternity but probably was five seconds. Circulation once again reached my brain. Obviously the best thing I could do was to go ahead and sit down. I spotted the only available seat in the classroom. Of course I was late and had to crawl over three W.A. Criswell wannabees two rows in front of "her." At the point where my bottom finally found its resting place, my mind immediately went into "search mode."

I knew this girl from somewhere, but where? The wheels in my brain were turning and churning. I remember that my brain was searching through all available files in order to make the proper identification. My first thought was about Sigrid Thornton. Who is Sigrid Thornton? Good question. She is one of the stars in the movie, *The Man from Snowy River*. It is one of my favorite movies of all time. I thought that Sigrid really was pretty. I thought to myself, "That girl looks just like Sigrid Thornton, but it couldn't be her. She lives in Australia." What would Sigrid be doing in Fort Worth, of all places? I could not figure out who she was, but I certainly knew her from somewhere. It was from somewhere in my past, but from where? For some reason my brain jumped to a folder called "Your Future Wife." The information in this folder contained a few scratched-out names with a skull and crossbones next to a couple of them. Of course what caught my attention was the flashing message that read, "This is the one!" The first time I laid eyes on her, I knew that she was the one for me. But I needed more data. I needed to do some research. I definitely was creating a convenient shortcut to be able to access this particular file immediately.

The roll was called in class. Yes, I definitely recognized the name, but from where? Thank the Lord, the first day of class was brief. All we did was review the syllabus. Then class was over. Well, you guessed it. I went up to her after class and gave her the best line I could think of at the time. I calmly and confidently asked, "Don't I know you from somewhere?" I definitely did better on my next lines. "Can I walk you home?" I asked. Karen had just been to the bookstore to buy books for her classes. She had numerous books to take home. I asked, "I'll carry your books for you. Those look heavy."

I know exactly what you are thinking at this point—two words: "stud muffin" or "smooth operator", or maybe six words, "Boy, am I starting to feel nauseous!" I could tell that she was smitten—at least with the outward appearance.

After class I offered to walk Karen home and carry her books, as any gentleman and scholar would do. And can you believe it? Karen had gone to my high school! Yes, of course. Now I remember. We attended a huge high school with about 3,000 students and ran with different crowds. She ran with the respectable people. All I remember about Karen from high school was that she really could swing those hips. I also remember that she was on the drill team. After high school, I attended Texas A&M University and Karen went to Baylor. Who, except God, ever would have thought that we would end up meeting each other once again as students at the same seminary in "Introduction to the Baptist Hymnal" class? OK, so I was wrong. This class was not going to be like a root canal, after all. By the way she wasn't blonde.

I had such a nice visit with her after class. Karen was just so beautiful that I went to her apartment that evening to give her a Hallmark greeting card just simply stating that I enjoyed meeting her. Once again I know what you are thinking. I delivered the card to her that evening—by hand, of course. Karen opened the door. She was happy to see me—I could tell. I also could tell that she definitely was interested. She was smiling, flirting, and pretending to be shy. Obviously I had interrupted her dinner, because the entire time we talked she had a ring of spaghetti sauce around her shy, cautious, and flirtatious lips. We said our goodbyes. Once again Karen told me "Thank you" for the card. We certainly planned to get together to talk some more. She shut the door; I left. Without a doubt I knew that Karen was the one for me—this Baptist seminary student, from my high school, who was on the drill team, a proud graduate of Baylor University, with a cute smile, nice hips, and the unforgettable spaghetti sauce on her face. Never say never.

All You Need Is Love

A few choruses of "Just As I Am" and "Amazing Grace" later, I graduated. Who said you needed Christian character to graduate from a Christian school? Now, what in the heck was I supposed to do? I never had been a pastor of a church. I knew as much about being a pastor and preaching as I did about urinary-tract infections. So, what was a person supposed to do with a master's degree in theology, a bachelor's degree in psychology, and no work experience in either field?

Oh, by the way, did I mention that I was engaged? So, let's summarize. I had two degrees, no job experience, I was engaged, and no money outside of $100 of graduation money. I had no job and no furniture. I did have a few clothes, my Pioneer stereo, and my Camaro. I had no place to live and nothing to eat. I did have drive and determination to prove to God and others that I was "somebody"!

I remember asking my wife's parents for her hand in marriage. I remember them asking me, "How are you going to take care of our daughter?" At that point I didn't have much to say. My only response was, "All you need is love." I only can imagine what they were thinking at that point. But they loved me and supported me anyway. They welcomed me into their family. Outside of my own dad, my father-in-law has had greater impact on my life than has any other man. To make matters worse my wife-to-be quit seminary and got a job making four dollars an hour teaching preschool in a church school. With a degree from Baylor University she was living at home and making four dollars an hour.

So, what did I do? I'll give you five seconds to guess. Congratulations. You guessed it. I hopped into another graduate program. When in doubt, go to graduate school. Amen? Three months later a church contacted me to be its pastor. Three months after that, I was married. I had a job, I had a wife, I had food, I had furniture, and I had a place to live. My wife and I spent the next five years serving in a little country church in Northeast Texas. What better place to prove to God and others that I was worthy of love, approval, and acceptance? What better place to earn back what I had thrown away? Don't stop now. Keep reading. Things are just starting to heat up.

Enough Is Never Enough

As a pastor I loved and served the people where I lived. To the very best of my ability I met all expectations. I did everything a pastor was supposed to do. I visited the sick. I performed weddings and funerals. I preached exciting, interesting, 20-minute sermons every Sunday. I visited the elderly. I visited new people in the community. I ministered to people in our community who went to different churches. I ministered to people in our community who did not go to church at all. I was active in our community. I even was elected to a public office. I did everything a good pastor was supposed to do. I was loved. I was successful. I wanted to prove to my new bride that I was worthy of her love. I wanted to prove to my in-laws that I was worthy to be in their family. Others were pleased with me. Certainly God must have been pleased with me. Maybe even my mother-in-law was pleased with me. You know what they say: "Behind every successful man is a good woman and a surprised mother-in-law."

I continued to work as a pastor and to work my way through my doctoral program. In my doctoral program I really began to excel. I was a respected person in my field of study—counseling and psychology. I was a respected and loved person in my church. I did everything a good pastor was supposed to do. I did everything a good student was supposed to do. I did everything a good husband was supposed to do. I did everything a good person was suppose to do. Driven by self-hatred, insecurity, inadequacy, and worthlessness—driven by my desire to please and to prove to others that I was somebody, I finally had arrived. On graduation day, when I received my doctoral degree, I looked back at my past accusers and abusers. I looked back with the face of victory. My heart was filled with pride. Unfortunately enough never was enough.

The Ultimate Step

Funny thing about "success", accomplishments, power, position, praise, recognition—enough never is enough. Interesting, isn't it? I needed to take one more step. What would be the ultimate step to prove to God, to others, and to myself that I was worthy? I'll give you five seconds to guess. Wrong. I did not enroll in another graduate program. Certainly, serving as a missionary in a former Soviet Union country would prove to God and to everybody else that I was a person of worth. What else would a person need to do? I wanted to please God. I wanted to earn back what I had thrown away. I wanted to earn His forgiveness. I wanted to prove my love to Him. This was exactly what my wife and I chose to do. We decided that we would be missionaries in the former Soviet Union. We knew the conditions would be very difficult. We knew life would be dangerous. We knew the language would be difficult. We knew the culture would be different. We knew that the country had no health care, but only my wife and I would be going. After six years of marriage, we still had no children.

The Ache for a Child

For six long and emotionally draining years my wife and I suffered through the anguish of infertility. This was the most difficult challenge we faced as a newly married couple. The church where I served as pastor did not provide insurance. I had great insurance as a staff member at the university where I taught and went to school. Unfortunately the insurance did not cover infertility. We spent our entire life savings trying to have a child. Month after month we literally flushed thousands of dollars down the toilet.

Not being able to have a child took a huge toll on my wife. Watching her suffer was difficult. She suffered in silence. Her main goal in life was to have children and to be a stay-at-home mom. This was her greatest goal and ambition—what she wanted most out of life. Month after painful month this dream never happened.

Mother's Days definitely were the worst Sundays of the year for my wife and for me. We always would have a special service at church in order to honor all the mothers who attended the service. We would give a rose to the mother who had the most years of experience and the greatest amount of wisdom (never the oldest mother). We presented a rose to the mother with the most family members present. We presented a rose to the newest mother and to the mother who traveled the greatest distance to be with her family. We then gave a carnation to all the women in the church as they left the service.

Every Mother's Day my wife sat by herself on the first row of the church. During the entire service she cried. She hid her tears from everyone and did a great job of it. I could see her suffering in silence. Even today as I write, my heart breaks as I remember her pain during this difficult time. I remember that Karen read a book entitled *The Ache for a Child.* She kept it on her nightstand and read from this book each night before she went to sleep. If ever a book had an appropriate title, it was this one.

Not only were Mother's Days difficult, taking the little brown bags to the nurses in the doctor's office always was quite humiliating for me. The same two nurses always sat behind a white counter listening to "Light Favorites" on the radio. The same nurse always slid open the glad window when I entered the office. "Is this your specimen for the month?" she always asked over the music as everyone in the waiting room listened and snickered. "Yes, this is the one," I would say. "This is my best batch yet. Take care of my boys," I called out as I left the office. I always thought, "Surely I could find a better way", like trusting God's timing. Maybe I'm not the only person who wants what he wants when he wants it.

We set a limit for ourselves financially. We reached that limit, passed the limit, scoped out some local banks to rob them, and then finally agreed that we would not spend any more money on infertility treatments or rob any banks. To be perfectly honest we knew we were going as missionaries to the former Soviet Union. What better place than there could be found to adopt a child? We contacted an international adoption agency and set the plan into motion. We could serve as missionaries for a while, adopt us a kid or two, and then get the heck out of there.

Not a Thermometer

My wife and I went through the grueling process of being appointed as missionaries. We were analyzed, synthesized, and homogenized. We were poked and prodded. They tore us completely down and then put us back together. They looked at every detail of our lives. They literally examined us from head to toe in every way. We finally made it through the difficult screening process and were appointed to serve in the former Soviet Union.

We quit our jobs. My wife quit her job as a teacher. I resigned as a pastor. We sold almost everything we owned. We had our clothes and some books left over to take with us. We sold one of our cars and sold our furniture for pennies on the dollar. Believe it or not, we still had a ton of junk left. We tried selling our junk; nobody really wanted it. We ended up giving it all away. All we had left were some clothes, our toiletry items, and some pictures we were taking with us overseas. We got rid of everything. We quit everything. We were ready to go except for three small boxes we were taking to storage in our Toyota Tercel, or what we called "our little tin can on wheels."

The day before my doctoral degree graduation, I was loading these last few boxes to take to storage when I noticed that I was the only one working. Where was my wife? I looked outside for her. I couldn't find her. She met me at the door. She had a strange look on her face. She grabbed my hand. She was shaking.

She led me back to the bathroom. She opened the bathroom door and turned on the light. She then picked up a plastic thing that looked sort of like a thermometer. She held it up in the air. Her hand was shaking uncontrollably. She began to cry and yelled out, "I'm pregnant!" What she held was an early pregnancy test. The color was bright pink—a positive! I couldn't believe it. The first thing out of my mouth was, "How did that happen?" We were so busy trying to get packed—trying to take care of all our business and trying to get loose ends tied. I don't remember even touching my wife. We were so busy. Obviously we weren't as busy as I had thought.

The next question I asked my wife was, "Now?" Soon we would be living in one of the most dangerous and hostile environments in the world with absolutely no medical care. How could we take a newborn to such a horrible place? My mind was racing a million miles an hour. I guess my wife saw that I was in a total state of frozenness. She asked, "Well, what do you think?" My senses finally took hold. I said, "I am the happiest person on earth!" We hugged for a long time and kissed. She gave me a crystal figurine. It said "#1 Dad" on it. She bought the figurine a long time ago in the hopes that, one day, she actually might be able to give it to me as a gift. Even now as I am writing, my heart is totally overwhelmed with thankfulness. My eyes are filled with tears of joy. My wife saw her doctor immediately. Sure enough, our suspicion was true. The thermometer was right.

Pregnant! I was shocked. I remember thinking that at least going to Russia would get us out of our Lamaze class. I remember one husband getting brutally beaten by his wife in his Lamaze class. The instructor informed each of the pregnant women how important walking was for their health and the health of the child. She told the dads that walking with their partners would help. The room was very quiet. Finally a man asked, "Can she carry a golf bag while we walk?" If that wasn't bad enough, a man spoke frantically into the phone, "My wife is pregnant. Her contractions are only two minutes apart!" "Is this her first child?" the doctor asked. "No, you idiot!" the man shouted. "This is her husband!"

I couldn't believe that my wife was pregnant! I was in complete and total shock. I soon would discover how the birth of a child will rock your world. Soon the performance would end. But before we get to the end of the performance, take an opportunity to "step into the spotlight" as you reflect on the questions on the next page.

You're in the Spotlight

Ah, the sweet taste of success! Few things exist like it. At least we have a moment in which we can temporarily feel good about ourselves. However, a down side exists to success and to the drive to excel. Expectations and meeting expectations always lead to more and greater expectations. Through rising to meet those expectations, more praise and recognition occurs. Then rise more, ever-increasing expectations. The cycle never ends. Enough never is enough. The drive for success temporarily soothes, but it also robs us of close, personal, intimate, honest, and trusting relationships with Christ and others. It robs us of personal health and well-being. It robs us of depending on the power of the Holy Spirit to guide us. What do you think? Take an opportunity to allow God to provide light, insight, and understanding as you reflect on the following:

1. How has "sweet success" helped to soothe the hurts and pains from your past? Do you agree that success is like a drug? Explain your answer.

2. Do you "hide" behind things such as knowledge, education, relationships, success, and/or the perfect "Christian" image? Do you think that this is a common problem? Explain your answer.

3. How do rising expectations lead to greater degrees of chaos and exhaustion in your life? Why is enough never enough?

4. Even in the midst of your undying attempt to meet and/or exceed ever-growing expectations, in the midst of your constant drive for success, in the midst of living to please others no matter what the cost, how has God continued to work miracles in your life in an attempt to draw you to Himself? What does this say about Him?

5. How has God proved to you that ultimately He is the One who is in control?

Stepping into God's Light

Heavenly Father,

Forgive us for seeking to meet our needs through what the world has to offer. Heavenly Father, forgive us for thinking that success, relationships, accomplishments, education, material possessions, or even ministry would satisfy our deepest, innermost needs. Nothing satisfies like You. No one satisfies like You. Give us, for You, a heart such as David's, who prayed: "As the deer pants for streams of water, so my soul pants for you, O God. My soul thirsts for God, for the living God (Ps. 42:1-2a). O God, you are my God. earnestly I seek you: my soul thirst for you, my body longs for you, in a dry and weary land where there is no water" (Ps. 63:1).

I confess that even in the writing of this material, I have worried about what people will think. Father, forgive us for being so controlled, so worried, and so driven by what other people think. Forgive us for being so fearful of rejection and criticism. Thank you for the reminder that no matter what happens in life, no matter how we are treated by others, You never will leave us nor forsake us.

Lord, thank You for your presence as we move into this next chapter. After all of the pretending, we thank You Lord that, as we will see in this next chapter, the show can finally end.

We pray in the Name of Jesus. Amen.

Chapter 8

The Final Episode

Pride goes before destruction, a haughty spirit before a fall (Prov. 16:18).

Through incredible determination, diligent work, and sacrifice, I reached a certain level of "success." In the eyes of others I was respected. I was driven to perform. I was driven to achieve. I was driven to excel. Because of my deep-seated feelings of inadequacy, selfish ambition, and shame, I was driven, forced, and compelled to be the best. Tragically my glory days were short-lived, as I saw everything I worked to build crack, crumble, and eventually fall apart.

Lights, Camera, Action!

In these final episodes we find an unexpected, cameo appearance by a group of unknown assailants. Each member of the group arriving on the scene is incredibly strong and muscular. Their arms are as large as my legs. They are unshaven. They are dressed in flannel shirts with the sleeves ripped off of both arms. They wear blue jeans and leather, steel-toed boots. They wear hard hats. They hold implements of various sorts—shovels, sledgehammers, and pickaxes. In only one year they completely destroy what has taken me 17 long and grueling years to build. As they work to totally destroy my beautiful Christian image, I see that they have a name for their crew. On the back of their shirts is written the name of their group. They call themselves "The Image Busters."

The Image Cracks

Needless to say, my wife's being pregnant changed our plans. What were we supposed to do? Neither of us had a job. We could not have the baby born in the former Soviet Union with one of the worst health-care systems in the world. We had sold everything we owned. We were homeless. We had no furniture. We had no food. We had no money. When our missions organization contacted us, I was busy writing on a piece of cardboard, "Will Preach for Food", and looking for some nice, comfortable bridges under which we could live.

The first thing our missions group did was to congratulate us on the good news. It proceeded to give us an offer we could not refuse. Our missions organization definitely emerged for us with flying colors. For the next nine months it put us on salary, which meant that we were covered by insurance as well. A family in a local church found out we needed a home. These people said that we could live in their furnished home free of charge while they were away on business. They specifically wanted a missionary family to stay in their home while they were away. We weren't quite a family and we weren't quite missionaries, but we were close on both counts. We were back in business. During this time of delay our missions organization required us to study Russian in preparation for our move overseas.

Through a local university my wife and I took an intensive Russian course. We met five days a week for five hours a day. This sounds like a lot, but for my wife and me, this time actually was like a vacation. We had been burning the candle at both ends. I had been serving in a church, going to graduate school, and teaching at the same university. My wife was teaching preschool. We had a lot going. This was the first time that we really had gotten to be together and to concentrate on only one thing in our lives. The house where we stayed was very nice—in fact, the nicest place we ever had lived in our married life.

Of course, during the entire nine months, I was freaking out. I could not believe that a baby was inside my wife's abdomen. To me this was an absolute miracle. I was amazed at every stage. I was amazed at every sonogram. I was totally amazed. I had no earthly idea about what was involved in having a baby. I was getting a real education.

The day of our final exam in our Russian class was when the baby decided to make an appearance. In my past I had used quite a set of excuses to get out of some final exams, but this reason was definitely the best reason I ever had used. I kept asking, "Are you sure the time is here?" "Well, how do you know?" We finally arrived at the hospital. The nurses examined my wife. They said she already was dilated to a five. Never in my life had I ever heard the phrase "dilated to a five." I quickly learned many new words and phrases that I never had heard before. On the monitor I could hear the baby's heartbeat—one of the most beautiful sounds I ever heard. Then the doctor broke her water. Time progressed hour after hour. My wife finally was dilated to a 10!

The medical staff decided that the time had arrived to get the show on the road. They told me to go and get dressed. I put on my robe. I put on my mask. I put paper coverings over my sneakers. I had my 35-mm camera hanging from one of my shoulders and my video camera hanging from the other shoulder. I was ready. I was the "Rambo" of the labor and delivery unit. I was ready to roll.

The doctor broke the water; my wife began to push. I was utterly and absolutely amazed. I helped coach my wife as she breathed just like we learned in our Lamaze class. I could see the top of the baby's head. I could not believe it. I was filming every second. My heart was racing 100 miles an hour. I could not believe what I was witnessing. I was filled with awe and amazement.

The head popped out. I could not believe my eyes. I was stunned. I was breathless. I was in total amazement. Soon the entire body was out and then, finally, the legs. I could not believe my eyes. The doctor held the baby high for everyone to see. A girl! Sarah Elizabeth was the most beautiful creation I ever had seen in my life.

I couldn't feel the floor under my feet. My feet did not touch the ground. My chest had expanded three or four times its normal size. I was filled with complete and total pride. I could feel tears of joy running down the sides of my cheeks. Immediately I knew that this was what life was about. This was life. I was oblivious to the entire world around me. All I could do was focus completely on my new, little daughter. I was totally mesmerized.

In 30 seconds I soaked in some of the most incredible and intense feelings that I ever had experienced until I heard the words, "Call the neonatal unit." *What do you mean by the neonatal unit?* I yelled within the deepest part of my soul. In 30 seconds total joy turned to total panic. The nurse taking care of our new, little daughter couldn't get her to breathe. The baby continued to stay blue. She was not breathing. She was not crying. The nurse called for the doctor. The medical team quickly sprang into action. The phone call went to the Neonatal ICU unit to bring a team as quickly as possible. I dropped both cameras. I was paralyzed with fear. I was filled with total panic. They brought in a special incubator and placed our daughter inside. My wife never even got to touch our new baby. Our daughter quickly was taken to NICU. I was with them every step of the way. They finally arrived at NICU. They told me to wait outside and that they would call for me. I paced back and forth, back and forth, back and forth. My mind and my heart totally were blank except for the picture in my mind and heart of our new baby girl. After what seemed like an eternity, they allowed me in the NICU. I remember praying, "Dear Lord, have mercy on our little girl."

I saw her: IV's in her head, IV's in her hands and feet, and tubes in her stomach. She was hooked up to a huge machine. She was fighting the doctors and nurses. She was fighting for her life. I remember the doctors and nurses saying, "Boy, she is an incredible fighter."

For hours on end I stayed in the NICU. I would not leave my little girl for any reason. I prayed like I never prayed in my entire life. The doctors stated that she was born with pneumonia and that her lungs were completely filled with fluid. The first 48 hours would be the most critical time. I stood by her side and stared. I could not take my eyes off her. I looked at every part of her from the top of her head to the bottom of her tiny toes. I remember every colored tube in her head, arms, and stomach. I learned everything about the machines that literally were keeping her alive. I monitored every reading and listened to every beep. I continue to pray every single second. I would gladly and immediately have traded every accomplishment, every diploma, every certificate, every bit of recognition, and even my very life for my daughter to be OK.

Finally the syringe that was hooked up to one of the many tubes began to fill with fluid. This was the first good sign that we saw in 24 hours. It meant that the fluid finally was beginning to drain from her lungs. During that critical 48 hours I do not remember sleeping, eating, or even going to the bathroom. I went to visit my wife in order to share with her the news about our daughter and to make sure that my wife was OK. As I told her the news, she began to cry. I held her as she cried. She kept saying, "I didn't even get to hold her."

The doctors and nurses worked around the clock. They gave our little girl the very best of care. The fluid continued to drain from her lungs. However, she still could not breathe on her own. We continued to wait and pray while she continued to fight. She definitely was a fighter. She definitely was determined to win. By the second day in the NICU her condition dramatically improved. She was going to make it. She was doing so well that she was able to breathe on her own. She stayed in NICU for a week of observation and to continue her rounds of medication. They gave us a room in the hospital in which we could spend time with our new daughter. After two days my wife finally got to hold our new little girl. She truly was a miracle child. The doctors and nurses at Baylor Medical Center were true miracle workers. We owed them a huge debt of gratitude. Thanks, friends.

I never had experienced such total joy and such total panic in such a concentrated period of time in my entire life. In the interim the image was damaged—a small, hairline fracture was visible on the furnace. For 17 years I had been working to build the ultimate Christian image. It was strong. It was impenetrable, or so I thought. I had built the ultimate image for all to see. I soon would discover that this only was the beginning of a series of damaging blows to the image I had spent a lifetime attempting to build and protect. Amazing what a difference love makes—and the birth of a new, little baby.

I Will Not Break

Two months later we were on a plane with our 2-month-old daughter and 16 footlockers. Two footlockers were filled with our clothes, toothpaste, soft toilet paper, taco-seasoning mix, hot sauce, cheese spread, and chips. Fourteen footlockers were filled with disposable diapers, baby toys, baby clothes, bottles, sippy cups, pacifiers, lotion, and 100 pounds of wipes. We left all our loved ones. We left everything and everyone we held dear. This was the most horrible day of our entire lives, but we couldn't back out. I *would* not back out. I said we were going to go; we went. Quitting was not an option. What would people think? Failure was unacceptable.

After a 24-hour trip we arrived at our destination: Kiev, Ukraine. We were exhausted. The airport was freezing; we immediately were met with open hostility. One of the flight attendants spoke both Russian and English; we asked her to help us. She said, "I am sorry, but that is not in my job description." We were left completely on our own. We had no idea what to do. Fortunately in the States we had studied some Russian.

Fortunately we were able to remember three or four words. Not one person in the entire airport would help us or even would answer our questions. I saw where other passengers were getting their passports checked, so we followed the crowd. I definitely knew how to follow the crowd. We were told that our passports and documents were not in order. I knew beyond a doubt that everything was in order. We were met with angry stares and questions of why we were there. Over and over again I told myself that I would not break. I would not be intimidated. I stood my ground; we finally were allowed to pass through to the place where we could get our luggage—16 footlockers weighing 70 pounds each. I pulled each of them off of the squeaky, run-down, rusted-out conveyor belt. I was amazed that our footlockers still were unopened and intact.

In the entire airport only one person spoke to us. Everyone else stood around the room and laughed at us. The one man that spoke to us asked for a $150 bribe to help with our luggage. In my best Russian I told him that he was absolutely crazy and to go away. He would not. He still kept trying to bargain. I told him I would pay him $50 to help. Once again he wrote a price of $150. I did not speak to him again.

I rented four luggage carts at a booth that rented carts, but I could not get the carts. I paid for my carts, but I could not get my carts. After I paid for the carts, they gave me a ticket. I had to take this ticket to the other side of the airport to get the ticket validated. Then I had to take the validated ticket back to the same booth where I originally paid to show the worker my validated ticket. He then gave me four tokens that I could put in the slot in order to get my carts. All the while I told myself that I would not break.

I loaded four footlockers on each of the four carts. Of course all the other Ukranian passengers had pushed and shoved in order to get in line in front of me. In the freezing, unheated terminal my wife waited and watched with our 2-month-old daughter. I could see the breath of my wife and that of our little girl. It was cold.

By that time numerous armed guards waited for me to reach the X-ray machines. They told me to put each piece through the X-ray machine. I unloaded all the carts and put each piece through the machine. Not one person helped. Not one person lifted a finger. As the footlockers passed through the X-ray machine, I had to take them off the conveyor belt at the back end and stack them. Then I went to the front of the X-ray machine and loaded more footlockers on the front end of the conveyor belt. I loaded 16 footlockers on the front end of the conveyor belt and removed and stacked 16 footlockers at the back end of the belt. What did every other person in the terminal do during this time? They laughed and joked at my expense. I told myself that I would not break. I told myself that I would not be intimidated. Not one person lifted a finger to help.

All of our footlockers had been checked through the X-ray machine. The customs officials then made me open 10 of the 16 footlockers to look inside. I continued to assure them that this was all of our personal things. They wanted to look inside anyway.

As I opened each of the designated footlockers, the customs officials proceeded to take everything out in order to look at every item. I then had to repack the 10 opened footlockers in order to shut them. They then told me to put all 16 footlockers back through the X-ray machine. I loaded the four carts with four footlockers on each cart. I wheeled the carts to the front of the conveyor belt. I unloaded the carts. I put the 16 footlockers on the conveyor belt at the front end of the X-ray machine and then unloaded the 16 footlockers at the back end of the conveyor belt.

Over and over I continued to tell myself that I would not break and would not be intimidated. Not one person did even the smallest thing to help me load and unload 16 footlockers weighing 70 pounds each onto the carts or onto the conveyor belts. After running all 16 footlockers back through the x-ray machine again, I then re-stacked the 16 footlockers on the rented carts—four footlockers per cart.

They passed me through customs. Total disgust can be a great motivator. I was NOT going to give up. On my way out one of the guards asked me why I did not pay the $100 in order to get help. I told him because the guy wanted $150. In broken English he replied, "Hmmm, this is robbery." They finally let one of our friends enter into the customs area. Until that time we were completely on our own. After two hours of lifting 70-pound footlockers, we finally made our way to the vans that would take us to our new home. Of course I had to load the footlockers onto the vans.

As I mentioned earlier, we arrived in the evening. We were freezing. In the dark we could not tell much about our new home. Anyway, our friends wanted to hear about our experience with the customs officials. By the time we had finished our heroic tale, we made it to our apartment building. We moved the 16 footlockers up four flights of stairs to our new apartment. On the outside our apartment did not look too awfully bad. We thought the nightmare was over. However we discovered that the nightmare was just beginning. The next morning we would be in for the shock of our lives.

The Image Begins to Crumble

When morning arrived, I wanted to check out our new surroundings. I wanted to explore the area that would be our home for the next year. We also needed some groceries. I opened the front door of our apartment only to be struck by a horrible odor—the smell of urine. Urine was everywhere—on the floor, down the halls in our building, and on the stairs. A shoeless drunk in an old, brown jacket and torn pants was passed out, asleep, and leaning against our door. He was using as a pillow his bottle of vodka wrapped in a Russian newspaper. I stepped over him and made my way down the four flights of stairs. I dodged puddles of urine all the way to the first floor, where yet another obstacle waited for me. Rats were everywhere. I did not seem to bother them. They did not even run away when I arrived. They continued to play on the small set of stairs that led out of the apartment building and into the parking lot.

Outside our building more rats played and had a great time. Garbage was piled around our apartment building. Obviously months had passed since it was picked up. Across the parking lot was an overgrown playground complete with weeds, broken swings, a rusted-out slide, and a broken picnic table covered with English profanity. The weather was cold, cloudy, and rainy. The day was dreary and depressing in every way.

I went to the market our friends told us about. The market was only a 10-minute walk from our apartment. It was a huge, open-air market with everything you possibly could want. Having a market so near to our apartment turned out to be a huge blessing during the winter months. Unfortunately I quickly learned that I did not know how to speak Russian very well at all. I needed eggs, cereal, milk, and bread. Fortunately I quickly found cereal and bread in one of the more than 100 small, 10-foot-by-10-foot booths called *kiosks.* Rows and rows of these made up the market. The major, time-consuming problem was going up and down each row and examining each item in each kiosk to try and find what I needed. Each kiosk had no rhyme or reason as to what was sold. I certainly did not see an area for cereal, an area for bread, or an area for milk. One kiosk might sell toys, tires, underwear, and grapefruit. Another kiosk might sell socks, cereal, coffee, and ceiling fans. Hence I was forced to search every kiosk or even worse, to speak Russian. I chose the worse of the two options. I tried to ask someone for what I needed. For some reason I could not remember the words for eggs and milk. So what did I do? You guessed it.

I made my way through the hundreds of people who were jam-packed together in this market and approached a person who I thought had a kind smile. She worked in one of the kiosks. She was an older, heavy-set woman. She wore a scarf on her head, a tattered dress and shoes, and a gray, dirty apron. I said "hello" in Russian. I then proceeded to cluck like a chicken, flap my wings, strut, peck, and pretend to lay an egg. I held my imaginary egg in the air and, in Russian, asked the question for "where"? She laughed as loud as anyone I ever had heard. Every one of her silver-capped teeth sparkled on an otherwise gloomy day. She pointed me in the direction I needed to go. Again I looked her straight in the eye, said the Russian word for "and", and proceeded to "moo" like a cow. I pretended to milk a cow by moving my clenched fists up and down in the air. Again she laughed, flashed that beautiful, silver smile and pointed me in the same direction as she had for the eggs. I said "thank you" and pushed my way through the crowd of people who had stopped to watch the crazy foreigner. I bought my milk and eggs and completed my shopping goals for the day.

After three hours at the market I forced my way through the crowds of people and pushed out into the street. Retracing my steps I eventually returned to the stairs of our building. I stepped over the rats, walked up four flights of stairs dodging the puddles of urine, stepped back over the drunk, and tightly secured the door behind me. I was, once again, safe inside our new home.

One Last Attempt to Hold Things Together

What do you get when you squeeze a lemon? You get what's inside. I definitely was being squeezed. Besides trying to survive, I was taking Russian lessons four days a week, four hours a day. This was my "job" for the next year—studying Russian. I no longer was a pastor. I no longer taught in a university. I no longer was a counselor. I no longer was a professional. I was a student with a hard-line, hard-nosed, communist teacher who longed for the days before "democracy" (actually "anarchy" would be more descriptive and accurate).

To get to my Russian class each day, I rode on the metro. At the time of the year we arrived, the weather was so cold outside that no cars in the entire city would start. At 6 every morning I walked 30 minutes to the closest metro station. I went underground to get to the platform where I would catch my train and allow my nose hairs to thaw. Many of the metro stations also served as bomb shelters. They were way underground. For an hour I rode the metro and then walked for another 30 minutes to get to my class by 8 a.m. Being from Texas I never had ridden a metro before. Now I rode one every day. Every day millions of people in our new city rode the metro. They would try to squeeze as many people in one train car as possible. Then they would try to get just one more person on board. I literally was being squeezed in every way. Since I was from Texas, I never had experienced a harsh winter. Snow literally fell inside the train while the blizzard raged outside. I wore layer after layer of insulated clothing and a coat that was so big, it could have housed a small family. I wore three scarves over my face, an insulated hat, and insulated, waterproof boots. On many days I had to stop and thaw out in one of the thousands of apartment buildings that plagued the landscape. The times when I could not feel my face, ears, and/or feet, I would stop, thaw out, and then continue on my journey.

At the same time I was being squeezed, my wife was going through a period of depression. She just had a baby, which certainly was one reason for her depression. Besides hormones gone haywire (talk about anarchy!), we left our family, friends, church, work, language, and culture. We left everything. We left all comforts and security. We lived in horrible conditions in a hostile environment. We were afraid. We masked our fear and directed our anger at each other. We verbally ripped each other to shreds. Hardly a day passed that we did not yell and scream at each other, harshly criticize each other, and lash out and bite with the poisonous venom of anger, resentment, and bitterness.

How bad were things? Recently a friend visited us for dinner. He asked if we ever experienced culture shock when we first arrived in that area of the world. After we finished laughing, my wife responded, "If I had known enough Russian to tell a taxi driver to take me to the airport, I would have taken our daughter and left for good. I just couldn't speak Russian well enough to do that." In other words, we were on the edge. However we did manage to have enough energy to keep up the good-Christian, good-missionary image when we met with our missionary friends. On the outside we were the good missionary family with no problems. On the inside we literally were falling apart at the seams.

I was being squeezed. What was on the inside literally was pouring out—anger, resentment, the unwillingness to forgive, criticism, harshness, and what seemed to be an insatiable desire to be in control. But I was not in control. I absolutely had no control. I was helpless. I was a helpless child desperately trying to survive in a hostile world. I was so afraid. Never had I known such fear. I was paralyzed with fear. The image not only was quickly crumbling around me, the image was absolutely and totally worthless. All of my degrees and accomplishments were 100-percent worthless. I couldn't stop my sinful attitudes, my sinful desires, and my need to be in control from pouring out of me. All of the ugliness on the inside emerged to the forefront. The ugliness of my sin stood before me for all to see. It stood before me, with clinched fists and grit teeth, standing ready for battle. In my entire life I never had seen such a revolting, nasty, despicable, obscene, disgusting, and grotesque monster. I was being squeezed. What was inside was pouring out and staring me in the face. I couldn't fake it anymore. I couldn't pretend anymore. I couldn't straddle the fence anymore. The pieces of my beautiful Christian image were falling apart faster than I could glue them back together. Something had to be done. I needed stronger glue and quicker fingers.

Broken

What we got was much better than glue. Deliverance for us occurred when we went to our first mission meeting in neighboring country. Oh, yes! Getting out of Ukraine was just what the doctor ordered—and not a moment too soon. This meeting occurred at the time just before total destruction. At this meeting for missionaries serving throughout Central and Eastern Europe, we heard some great preaching. We listened to other missionaries who were struggling with some of the same problems. We also talked to a Christian counselor. This was great. It was the first time we told anyone that we were having problems. It was like a weight was lifted off of our shoulders. How great not to have to pretend anymore! I had been pretending for so long, I had forgotten what it was like to be open and honest without worrying what others might think. We got our feet back on the ground. My wife and I made peace with each other and with God. After many tears and much forgiveness, we finally were back on the same team. When we returned to our place of service, we were new people. We even started to enjoy where we lived. We even found the beauty in the country and in the people. We actually started to like Ukrainians. We couldn't believe it! After 11 months, we could speak the language (sort of); we could get around; we could survive. Strangely enough, we did not want to leave.

Unfortunately this is exactly what we had to do. The time arrived for us to leave. We had completed our language-school requirements. Now time had arrived for us to move to our final destination. Our new place of service would be in an even more difficult, more hostile, and much poorer part of the former Soviet Union. Lord knows that we did not want to leave. We did not want to leave our friends, our church, and everything that was comfortable. Once again we packed all of our belongings into 16 footlockers.

The plan was for me to travel 24 hours by van. My wife and our 14-month-old daughter were to travel by plane. We decided that a 24-hour trip with no places to stop, no places to use the bathroom, no places to eat, hassles, and bribes at every town and border crossing would be much too difficult a trip for a baby and a wife that was two-months' pregnant. Oh, by the way, I forgot to tell you that we were expecting again. After the mission meeting, getting our feet back on the ground, and deciding that we weren't headed for divorce court, my wife and I started to have sex again. I sure am thankful for good preaching, for our fellow missionaries, and for good, Christian counselors.

The day at the airport was dreary. It was foggy, rainy, and very cold, just like the day we arrived. The dense fog delayed the Aeroflot flight, so we waited and waited and waited. Four hours passed; we still waited.

Our daughter was climbing the walls. We decided to go upstairs to a room that was reserved for traveling passengers with children. It had some baby beds and some regular beds with pillows. It also had some chairs. It was comfortable.

At the moment we stepped into this room, my wife began to bleed. With a look of total panic she looked at me and said, "I'm having a miscarriage. We are losing the baby." I never will forget the blood or my wife's look of panic and shock. I remember her saying over and over, "We are losing the baby." I held on to our 1-year-old while my wife rushed to the bathroom to try to stop the bleeding. When she returned, she was crying. She sat down, placed her head on my shoulder, and continued to cry. Over and over she said, "We lost the baby. We lost the baby. We lost the baby." Everything happened so suddenly.

I did not know what to do. We were helpless. We could not even call on anybody. We had to have a special phone card in order to call from the airport. We certainly did not want to go to the hospital. In our area of the world, going to the hospital to receive medical care was not an option. All I could think of was to get my wife a change of clothes and to pray. Our luggage was out in the car. I made sure that my wife was OK to sit and look after our daughter for the few moments I was away.

I walked down the stairs and through the airport terminal. I made my way outside to the parking lot. All the while I was praying, "Dear God, I don't know what to do. Should we go back to our apartment? Should my wife and child continue on their journey? I have no one to call. I have no one to ask. Help me, God. I beg you."

I found some clothes for my wife. I remembered to bring all of the necessary items. I closed her bags. I locked the car and began walking back to the terminal. Again, in the rain, the fog, and the cold, I prayed, "Dear God, I don't know what to do. Should we go back to the apartment? Should my wife and child continue on their journey? Should I put our entire trip on hold? All of our things are packed at the apartment—no beds, no dishes, nothing. What should I do, God? I am totally depending on you. I beg you for an answer. I beg you for wisdom. Please help me, God."

When I entered the terminal, I heard the call for my wife's flight after six hours of waiting. Was this the answer to my prayers? I made my way back to the room in which my wife and daughter were staying. I watched our daughter while my wife went to change in the bathroom. When she returned, she said that she was able to stop the bleeding. I asked her if she would be able to make the trip with our daughter. She said she could. I took as an answer to my prayer the announcement over the intercom. Once again I prayed: "Dear God, I don't know if I am doing the best thing or not. I am trusting in you. I am trusting that you will take care of my wife and my little girl. I am trusting in you, God, to keep the bleeding under control. I have no other option but to trust You."

I went and got my wife's luggage out of the car. We made our way to the customs area and said goodbye. I tried to tell the customs people about my wife's condition. I asked whether I could help her to the plane. They responded, "Absolutely not!", and ordered me to stand behind the line away from my family. Never did I want to commit murder than at that very moment. I gave my wife and daughter a hug goodbye. They left to go to a separate room in order to wait to be taken to the plane. I walked outside the terminal, where I could see them through a window. They were waving goodbye. They waved their final goodbyes. That was the last I saw for a while of the two most important people on earth to me.

I retrieved my Russian-made car and began driving home to our apartment. Halfway home I pulled over on the side of the road and stopped the car. In anger I slammed both hands down on the steering wheel. How could I have sent my family away during the time they most needed me? At that point the "Christian" image was destroyed completely. God was completely and totally in control. I sat in silence with only the sounds of the windshield wipers, cars racing by, the rain, and my tears. I was completely humbled. I was completely helpless. I was completely dependent on Him. I was broken. I had no other choice but to wait on Him and to totally trust in Him. I hated every minute of it. I later saw that *broken* was the place God wanted me all along.

When I returned to the apartment, I called everyone that sprang to my mind, including our Ukrainian doctor. He was the only doctor we knew in all of Kiev, a city of about four-and-a-half million people. On the phone I spoke to his wife. She said that he was out of town for two weeks. In other words, if my wife had returned with me to our apartment, she would not have been able to see a doctor at all. I also called my friends who were waiting at the airport in Moldova for my wife and daughter to arrive. I explained the entire situation. As things turned out, our friends knew the doctor who worked for the American Embassy.

Once the plane landed, this group immediately took my wife to see this doctor at the hospital. With the only ultrasound machine in all of Moldova the doctor performed an ultrasound to determined exactly what had happened to her. The doctor revealed that my wife still was pregnant but that the womb contained a lot of blood. The doctor advised my wife to have an immediate abortion because of the fear that she would hemorrhage to death. Of course my wife said this was not an option. The doctor then recommended that my wife get to Germany for medical care as soon as possible because little prenatal care existed in Moldova.

"Get to Germany as soon as possible" was exactly what we needed to hear. Before our insurance would kick in, we needed to have a recommendation from a doctor in our area of the world. This was policy. Immediately our missionary organization stepped in.

Karen and Sarah were careflighted to Germany, where my wife received excellent care. The doctors in Germany clarified that the blood in my wife's uterus was from a twin which had died. Twins? Who knew? The danger of losing the other baby still existed. They informed us of the danger of the dead baby being flushed out of the womb and taking the other baby with it. All we could do was to wait and pray. Again I had absolutely no control. All I could do was to depend on God and to wait. I was totally helpless.

Because of my wife's serious condition, she stayed in Germany for two months. Karen and Sarah returned to Moldova for several months. Then Karen was sent to America at the end of her eighth month of pregnancy. For five months total we were separated during the pregnancy and post-delivery time. Meanwhile I moved our things to our new home in Moldova and began my new work as a professor teaching at a theological seminary. I had to do something. I was going crazy. Actually I wasn't going crazy. I was seeing things clearly for the first time in a long time.

During this time of separation I was completely alone in one of the poorest, most pitiful countries in all of Europe. During this time God chose to show me a picture of my "Christian" life, or what I thought was living the Christian life. During this time of separation, humility, helplessness, and total dependence on God, He showed me a picture of the trap of sin and selfishness that held me firmly in its grip. During this time my beautiful Christian image was completely destroyed. The only thing that mattered was the health of my wife and new little baby growing in her womb. My skills, training, degrees, and certifications meant absolutely nothing. When I was totally vulnerable, God showed me that the time had arrived for the show to end. I wrote about all these events and feelings in the "lost" journal that my missionary colleague found and that I mentioned earlier.

So there you have it. After 17 years of building the image, striving for success, and desperately trying to earn love, approval, and acceptance, the performance finally ended. There at the bottom in the poorest country in all of Europe God finally had me where He wanted me. I was broken. For many years I simply would not break. I lived with the lies, "I can do it, and if I can't do it, I'll try even more diligently." Brokenness says, "I can't do it." Brokenness says, "Lord, You'll have to do it. You'll have to live the Christian life through me." During that time of brokenness God showed me who I was. In that time of brokenness I discovered my biggest problem. My biggest problem was me. I have since realized that when we are broken is when God can use us.

You're in the Spotlight

God's Word definitely is right. When you build on a foundation other than Christ, in only a matter of time everything will fall. God literally is opposed to the proud. He will humble those He loves. If you think you are standing tall—if you think you are secure and successful, watch out! Before you move to the next section entitled "Behind the Scenes", allow God to bring to light some insights regarding your own, personal, "Christian" image.

1. Describe your beautiful "Christian" image. How do you want others to perceive you? How are you attempting to influence what other people think about you? In other words what are those things you desperately are striving to hide?

2. How has God used devastating circumstances and/or difficult people to bring you to the very end of who you are? What was the result? How did you respond? In what ways did you try your best to remain strong?

3. In those most difficult times, what were the greatest lessons you learned? Write them out. Share with a good and trusted friend these incredible insights.

4. How did you cry out to God? Get out a sheet of paper or fire up the computer. Remember and record some of your prayers you prayed during those most devastating times. How did God answer those prayers?

5. What was finally surrendering control like for you? Describe what happened when you not only received Christ as Savior of your life but also made Him Lord of your life.

Stepping into God's Light

Heavenly Father,

In the Old Testament You talked about the Jews being a stubborn and stiff-necked people. After reading this last chapter we are amazed at how stubborn we can be. You moved heaven and earth to bring us to the point You needed us to be—once again dependent on You. You were right when you said, "Pride comes before a fall" (Prov. 16:18). The circumstances You used to break us were painful and devastating. But thank You, Lord, for using the tough times of life to draw us closer to You.

Lord, please go with us as we go "Behind the Scenes" in this next chapter and examine our lives and hearts at a much deeper level. Hold up the mirror and allow us to see ourselves for who we really are. Allow us to see ourselves through Your eyes.

We pray in the name of Jesus. Amen.

Chapter 9

Behind the Scenes

Examine yourselves to see whether you are in the faith; test yourselves (2 Cor. 13:5).

What happens when the show ends? Everybody goes home. Some lucky folks, however, may get to go backstage and—up close and personal—meet the main characters. They may get to go "behind the scenes" and hear many details of how the performance was put together. God took me "behind the scenes" to take a deeper look at what was going on in my Christian life. During the five months of separation from my family, God showed me how and why I was literally driven, compelled, forced, and even addicted to performing "good" and "Christian" activities. During the time of separation God showed me the "big lie" and how this lie was separating me from Him and from others. Most importantly God showed me how to break free from the deadline performance trap hindering my ability to love and to devote myself to Him and hindering my ability to love, accept, and forgive others. God showed me; now, I'd like to show you. Please accept this invitation to take a moment to go "behind the scenes."

Oh, by the way, my wife gave birth to the surviving twin—another beautiful, blonde-haired, curly-headed girl. We named her Abigail Grace. Now, at age 7, she thinks her daddy is wonderful!

Living a Lie

I'm amazed that such a complicated, self-glorifying, self-righteous, religious system can be boiled down to a simple lie: **I am not worthy to be loved.** Behind all the accomplishments, achievements, successes, religious activity, and the "Christian image" always is a lie. Tragically the conclusion we draw from this lie leads us, or those caught in the performance trap, to a second devastating lie: **I must prove that I am valuable, important, and worthy of love.** The very instant we began to strive to prove that we are worthy, religion is born, hypocrisy is born, self-righteousness is born. This always is the beginning of the end. This always is the point in which we attempt to pour "old wine into new wineskins." In the process a third lie is born: **We begin to believe the lie that we can be good by doing good. Hence, the more we do for God and for others, the better we are. As a result our "Christian lives" lurch completely out of control.**

The Fruit of Performance

Once again, I hear what you ask, "Aren't we supposed to do good deeds, bear fruit, and for these to be evidence of genuine faith in our lives?" This is an excellent question. The answer is found in the difference between performance and obedience. Performance has everything to do with success. Obedience has everything to do with character. You and I are most concerned with appearances; God is most concerned with the motives in our hearts. Determining whether you are trapped in performance or following through in obedience is simple. Just ask yourself, "Who is the one in control—you or God?"

When you are obedient, God is in control; the fruit of the Spirit—love, joy, peace, patience, kindness, gentleness, goodness, and self-control—always are present. When you are wrapped up in performance, you are in control and always have the fruit of performance—pride, success, resentment, lust, control, secret sins, fear, a negative and critical spirit, discouragement, and exhaustion. Let's inspect this fruit before we move to an opportunity to "go behind these scenes" and examine the evidence of performance in your own life.

Pride: We can do good and be good independently of God. In other words, our successes, accomplishments, achievements, and position prove our value and worth. We are good and special because of what we do for God.

Success: Success represents all of our accomplishments, achievements, good deeds, and godly activities we do in an attempt to earn favor, love, approval, recognition, and acceptance from God and others. Success is what is most important. Character, integrity, purity, holiness, and obedience no matter the cost are not our main concern.

Resentment: Resentment is the unwillingness to forgive while we hold on to our right to punish. In other words we believe we have every right to be angry, to punish, and to blame. We hold on to our hate and hurt from the past while we blame God and others for not making things exactly how we want them to be.

Lust: Lust goes far beyond sexual lust. Lust is the desire for all of the things we do not have. Lust is the heart of dissatisfaction and discontent. We want what others around us have. We want the most, the biggest, and the newest we can get.

Control: Our lives, our possessions, our relationships, our time, our agendas, our dreams, our desires, our ambitions, and our relationships are ours to control.

Secret sins: Whenever we are the ones in control, secret sins always are present. Unfortunately we are deceived into thinking that our secret sins hurt only us and no one else. The truth is that any time we take control and do whatever is required to meet our own needs, God's power, His Spirit, and His working in and through our lives grinds to a halt.

Fear: Whenever we strive to please others and measure up to their expectations, fear always is present. Fear of failure, fear of rejection, and fear of criticism keep us imprisoned by the need to please and to meet others' expectations.

A negative and critical spirit: We become our own worst critics. We literally beat ourselves into submission to keep going, not quit, strive for success, and strive to be the best. Of course we never are satisfied. Nothing less than perfection is acceptable. Mistakes, sins, and shortcomings are unacceptable. The tragedy is that we treat others the same way. If others do not measure up to our rigid and extremely high expectations, they will experience firsthand the way we treat ourselves—harsh criticism, judgment, punishment, and the demand to get on with the program.

Discouragement: Discouragement always is present. For some reason we never understand that we are valuable and worthy of love. The truth is that the world doesn't have enough accomplishments, achievements, or successes to ever satisfy our empty and hurting souls. Only Christ and Christ alone can meet our deepest and innermost needs. His value and love are gifts that we must accept and enjoy, not earn.

Exhaustion: In my opinion this is the most tragic of all. In our desire to promote ourselves, we neglect our most important relationships with Christ and others. We are alone and isolated. We are successful but unloved. We succeed in the world but fail at home. We constantly are on the go. We are overwhelmed. We never slow down. We run on fumes. We have been doing this for so long that it seems normal. We are just too tired and too busy to love. We never take the time to stop and realize that rejuvenation, renewal, true value, and true worth only are discovered as we invest in our most important relationships.

> ***On a Personal Note . . .***
>
> *Whenever others and especially the Lord get the leftovers, we become exhausted, discouraged, and disobedient—no matter how successful we may appear to be on the surface. If you are exhausted, angry, discouraged, mean, and nasty in private and syrupy sweet in public, then obviously you are the one in control. If you are in control, then Christ is not Lord.*

Actor or Authentic?

Now your turn is here to examine whether or not the fruit of performance are part of your life. Who is in control—you or God? Are the "great" things you are doing for God and others for His glory or for your glory? Are you an actor or authentic? Are you fake or faithful? Read each of the following statements in the "Make-Believer's Checklist." Place a check in the appropriate column. Don't worry. Writing in your book is OK. You may have a difficult time actually placing a check mark in your book. If you are concerned that others might see the answers you marked in your book, go ahead and mark statements 39 and 49 as "True." Good luck. I'll meet you when your exercise is over.

The Make-Believer's Checklist

	True	False
1. I try as diligently as I can to be the best I can be.	______	______
2. When others fail or make mistakes, they deserve to be punished.	______	______
3. I work diligently to prove my love for God.	______	______

	True	False
4. The more I do for God, the more He is pleased.	______	______
5. I rarely if ever recognize or confess my sins.	______	______
6. Often my quiet times are a "check-off" on my list of things to do.	______	______
7. I am exhausted most of the time.	______	______
8. I am too busy.	______	______
9. I often am critical of myself and others.	______	______
10. I get angry and frustrated when things don't go my way.	______	______
11. I prefer being in control	______	______
12. I am competitive.	______	______
13. I often gossip about others.	______	______
14. I hold on to hurts, failures, and regrets from my past.	______	______
15. Forgiving is difficult for me.	______	______
16. I desire recognition and praise for my good works—at least a simple thank-you.	______	______
17. When times get tough, I pull myself up by my bootstraps and hang in there.	______	______
18. Compared with others, I am doing pretty good.	______	______
19. I want to do something important in life and be somebody important in life.	______	______
20. I enjoy talking about the great things I've done for God or hearing someone else talk about the great things I've done. This makes me feel proud.	______	______

	True	False
21. I often feel inadequate, insecure, or discouraged..	______	______
22. Trusting others is difficult for me.	______	______
23. I fear rejection; I'm sensitive to criticism.	______	______
24. I am afraid to fail and to make mistakes.	______	______
25. I am anxious and worry about many things.	______	______
26. Admitting that I am wrong is difficult.	______	______
27. I sometimes lie in order to protect myself.	______	______
28. I am not the same in the privacy of my own home as I am in church on Sundays.	______	______
29. I am driven to excel, succeed, and achieve.	______	______
30. I expect others to do what I say or do what I want, or I get upset.	______	______
31. To get things done I trust in my own abilities.	______	______
32. I rarely am satisfied. I want bigger, better, or newer.	______	______
33. I want others to be pleased with my performance.	______	______
34. Saying "no" is very difficult for me.	______	______
35. Being right is very important to me.	______	______
36. I have secret sins in my life.	______	______
37. I just can't seem to relax or to slow down.	______	______
38. To be of value I must be doing something productive.	______	______

	True	False
39. What others think of me is very important to me.	______	______
40. If others knew the real me, they wouldn't like what they see.	______	______
41. On the surface I appear to be a devoted, obedient Christian, but I know that I am the one in control.	______	______

Some General Comments

How did you do? First of all, if you marked several of the blanks as "True", this may indicate that you are attempting to earn God's love, approval, or favor through your own efforts. You may be asking, "What do you mean by 'several'?" This really is for you to decide. If you want me to decide for you, if you checked 10 or more as "true", I'm glad you are reading this book. The next chapters will be of utmost importance to you. Falling into the trap of thinking that God certainly must be pleased with you because of all the many things you do for Him is easy. You may think that He certainly will bless you with great things and a great life because of your acts of service for Him. However, what happens when life's storms arrive in your life? Does this mean that God does not love you or is punishing you or doesn't care or cannot be trusted?

Secondly, several blanks marked as "True" might reflect your striving to earn love, approval, or recognition from others. You easily can fall into the trap of living in order to please others. Sure, when others are pleased, they tend to give you what you want. The down side is that people are fickle. Pleasing everybody all the time is impossible. The result is that you often are left feeling disappointed, discouraged, frustrated, and resentful.

Finally, several blanks marked "True" may indicate where you place your trust. You may be depending on your own strengths and abilities to control your own life and relationships. You constantly are tired, drained, and exhausted because you're taking on way more than the Lord ever intended and are refusing to trust in Him, go to Him, refill, relax, recuperate, and renew.

On a Personal Note . . .

If the checklist you just completed describes you, then the following chapters will help you. Certainly they helped me. Thanks for the opportunity to examine our lives and our hearts together, since both of us seem to be a little more controlling and less trusting than we would like to be or to admit. I guess, by this point, both of us realize that we are a little less genuine than we would like to be. Thanks for being honest. Honesty is the first and most important step to bringing an end to all the performing and pretending. Before you move to the next section entitled "Bringing Down the Curtain", take an opportunity for God to shed some light into your life as you step into His spotlight in the next section.

You're in the Spotlight

Amazingly I realized that my entire Christian image—the heart of my pretending to be something I wasn't—stemmed from the lie, "I am not worthy to be loved, so I must prove that I am." I sure wasted a lot of time, trouble, and effort for one little distortion of the truth. As you examine the following questions, allow God's truth to expose some of the lies you may be harboring in your heart:

1. I have trouble believing that the heart of shame and the drive to perform and please is a lie. We both have something in common. We both believe the lies that "We are not worthy to be loved, so we must prove that we are." What may be some other lies that keep you in hiding?

2. Look at "Actor or Authentic?" once again. What fruit of performance are most evident in your life? How do these fruit differ from the fruit of the spirit in Galatians 5?

3. How many statements did you mark "true" when you took the "Make-Believer's Checklist"? Did it surprise you? What does your score say about your relationship with Christ?

4. Go back and star the checklist's top five characteristics with which you struggle the most. List and describe in greater detail these characteristics.

5. After you take the checklist, with whom are you willing to share your results? What are the most significant insights you would share? Remember, honesty is the first and most important step to "bring the curtain down" on the show.

Stepping into God's Light

Heavenly Father,

You know exactly how I developed the "Make-Believer's Checklist." I simply looked in a mirror and wrote down everything I saw. I was an expert in pretending. I was an expert in hiding. Life seems so much easier when you hide. We know that this is just another big lie. We know we sacrifice open, honest, genuine relationships with You and others whenever we hide. We know what we hide makes us unhealthy. We know our secrets make us sick. Thank You for the mirror You held up before us in this chapter. Thank you for identifying the many, many different ways we hide. Father, break through our fake, candy-coated Christianity. Unlock our prisons of artificial faith and set us free.

Heavenly Father, thank You for going with us as we move into this next chapter. Thank You for reminding us of some key steps to help us "G.E.T. R.E.A.L" in our relationship with You and others. By Your grace we don't have to hide anymore!

We pray in the Name of Jesus. Amen.

Chapter 10

Bringing Down the Curtain

Rather, we have renounced secret and shameful ways; we do not use deception, nor do we distort the word of God (2 Cor. 4:2).

Through some very difficult circumstances God definitely brought the curtain down on my little documentary. Trust me; this was a tough way to learn. I since have learned less painful ways to discover a more authentic Christian life. If you desire hope and healing from hypocrisy—if you desire to cancel your personal show—the first step always is to re-focus your attention, to re-focus the spotlight on Christ through repentance. Our greatest need as "Make-Believers" is repentance—and not just from the "bad" things we do. Our greatest need as "Make-Believers" is repentance from our own goodness. Whenever we perform, our focus always is on ourselves and on our audience. The result is living the "Christian life" without Christ. It is called religion. I will vouch from personal experience. Few things are more unlikely on earth than good people repenting from their own goodness. More often than not tragic circumstances are required to bring us back to who we really are and to re-focus us on Christ. Or, you can consider the following suggestions to "G.E.T. R.E.A.L." in your relationship with Christ.

Get Down and Get Humble.
Expose True Lies.
Take It to the Streets.

Re-Fill 'Er Up.
Escape the Madness.
Accent Accountability.
Love More and Expect Less.

Get Down and Get Humble

Humble yourselves, therefore, under God's mighty hand, that he may lift you up in due time. Cast all your anxiety on him because he cares for you (1 Pet. 5:6-7).

And when you pray, do not be like the hypocrites, for they love standing in the synagogues and on the street corners to be seen by men. I tell you the truth, they have their reward in full. But when you pray, go into your room, close the door and pray to your Father, who is unseen. Then your Father, who sees what is done in secret, will reward you (Matt. 6:5-6).

The first step toward a more genuine relationship with Christ is to turn from focusing so much on ourselves and focusing our attention on Christ as Lord. In other words, the time has arrived for you to step outside the spotlight and allow Christ to have center stage. If you want to hide something, hide this truth in the depths of your heart: your success, your needs, and your feelings are not what are most important in life.

One of the great tragedies in our society today is that Christians and non-Christians are exactly the same in their drives for self-fulfillment and self-satisfaction and fuel these drives in much the same ways. Hope does exist. For Christians, however, repentance refocuses our attention on God and away from ourselves.

Repentance allows God to clean us from the inside out. If we were honest, we would admit that, more often than not, our Christian lives are all about us—our goodness, our agenda, and our success. Throughout the Old and New Testaments God continually calls His own people to repentance.

Tragically God's people have many reasons for refusing to repent. The number-one reason we refuse to repent is because we are a prideful people. We refuse to humble ourselves, surrender control, and recognize Christ as Lord. Unfortunately pride is not the only reason we refuse to repent. We refuse to repent because:

We substitute remorse for repentance. Do we feel sorry about using God and others for our own personal benefit? You better believe we do. Do we feel sorry about stepping outside the boundaries of our relationship with Christ to meet our own personal needs? Most certainly. But, do we feel sorry to the point that we confess our hypocrisy, control, manipulation, selfishness, and secret ambition as sin and consistently live for Christ as Lord no matter the cost and no matter the circumstances? That is a different question.

We substitute self-improvement for repentance. We feel genuinely sorry. We vow to change. We promise never to do those things again. We determine in our mind, heart, and soul to do better and to try more diligently. Then we strive even more diligently to be the very best we can be in every area of life.

We are too busy to repent. Someone has said that "a busy life is an unexamined life." I agree completely. We can be so busy striving for significance, meeting an endless list of expectations, and fulfilling an endless list of responsibilities that we never even think that in the process, we are killing our most important relationships. A huge hindrance to repentance is the lie that "busy means important." The truth is that a Christian trapped in the busyness of life does not experience love, joy, peace, satisfaction, or contentment. A Christian trapped in the busyness of life experiences frustration, exhaustion, resentment, and hopelessness.

We think that no need exists to repent if others are pleased with us. We do what we are supposed to do. We work diligently to do what is expected of us. We not only perform well, we excel. We learn how to do the right things and say the right things. We learn how to work the system and work it well. But we don't live by the Spirit. We do not enjoy a consistent, growing, submissive relationship with Christ. We basically try our best and even dedicate our lives to fulfilling our own expectations and the expectations of others. Successful people, good people, taxpayers, and churchgoers don't need repentance.

We refuse to repent because the rewards are too great. When we are in control of our own Christian lives, the rewards are huge. The earthly rewards are huge. The rewards from the world are success, recognition, position, power, status, comfort, material rewards, and temporary relief of self-hatred and hurts from the past. The rewards from the church also are huge. The rewards from the church are recognition, power, status, respect, and the opportunity to say, "Look what a good, Christian person I am." In other words we earn the right to say, "Look at us. We are successful in the world and in the church. We must be good people." We earn the right to believe about ourselves that we are valuable, significant, important, and successful. One of the biggest and deadliest addictions on earth is the addiction to self-glorification. Enough never is enough.

We deny the costs of refusing to repent. The earthly rewards of a performance-based, works-based system of religion are huge. However, the costs of this self-glorifying, self-centered system are nothing short of devastating. The cost is the loss of everything that is most important in living the Christian life. The price is resentment, bitterness, hopelessness, discouragement, frustration, pride, and self-reliance. The price is the absence of joy, peace, contentment, and rest. The greatest cost is the absence of love. The cost is love—our love for Christ and our love for others, especially those who are closest to us. The cost is ensuring that our self-centered, self-glorifying, religious system of do's and don'ts is passed on to future generations.

We refuse to repent because we hate to admit we are wrong. The more religious you are, or prideful, the less likely you are to repent. For example my wife says that I was born without a sense of direction. I have become lost in more countries, including the U.S., than I ever would like to admit. On the other hand my wife never gets lost. I hate when she is right and I am wrong. Recently we drove across town. Guess what? I got lost. I had no clue where I was going. The last thing I wanted was for my wife to know that I was lost. She calmly and kindly said, "Honey, if you take this next street to the right, we can get back to the highway and back going in the direction we need to go." In my usual gruff tone I replied, "I know where I'm going. If I need your help, I'll ask for it!" By the time we arrived at our destination two hours late, everybody else at the party was packing up to go home. Our nature simply is not to admit we are wrong, or that we need help, or that we are going in the wrong direction.

The opposite was true for Patsy Capps. She knew her only hope was to depend on God in her fierce battle against cancer. Patsy said, "Cancer brought me to my knees—exactly where God wanted me to be." She said on her knees she caught a life-saving glimpse of God. She said picturing God was like viewing the Lincoln Memorial. Just as with Lincoln she pictured God sitting on His throne but never saw His face. She knew He was too holy for her to see His face, but she knew she was seeing God. She said this glimpse of His awesome majesty and holiness each day saved her during her two-year battle with chemotherapy and cancer. Now, five years later, she has a one-percent chance of the cancer ever returning. I like how she ended her testimony. She said, "Even with my cancer in remission, I still am on my knees each and every day."

In our overly busy, self-centered, and success-driven lives, we have lost our awe of God. One of my favorite ministry opportunities occurred when war broke out in Kosovo in 1999. I joined fellow missionary colleagues in ministering to those who lost everything—including the ones they loved the most. As we served 36,000 meals a day, the days were long and tough. During this difficult and rewarding time of ministry, we worked and played diligently. I stayed with another missionary couple who, since the day I arrived, had been planning a surprise for me. Finally they said, “Steve, we want to show you something.” We got in their Land Rover and traveled outside the city past the French checkpoint and past the Italian checkpoint to a huge ravine with cliffs on each side. The cliffs were so high that when I looked outside the vehicle windows, all I could see was solid rock. We finally reached our destination and got out of the vehicle. Out of the solid rock was a stream of water falling several hundred feet to a pond below. As the water flowed, a rainbow arched over the fast-running stream. The wife said, “We love this place. Just like the stream cuts through solid rock, God’s love can break through the hardest of hearts. This is our prayer for this country.” Then husband and wife began to sing. “Our God is an awesome God. He reigns from heaven above.” I joined in the chorus. I never had experienced such a real glimpse of the awesome majesty of God.

I invite you to catch a glimpse of God according to His Holy Word.

He is the Alpha and Omega (Rev. 1:8, 4:8).
He is the Almighty (Hag. 2:6-9).
He is the Christ, the Son of God (John 20:27-31).
He is Our Champion (Rom. 8:34).
He is the Wonderful Counselor (Isa. 9:6-7).
He is the Creator (Col. 1:15-17).
He is Everlasting (Heb. 1:10-12).
He is Forgiveness (1 John 1:9).
He is Our Friend (John 15:14-16).
He is God’s Only Son (John 3:16).
He is Heir to All Things (Heb. 1:1-2).
He is Holy and Righteous (Rev. 15:3-4).
He is Our Hope (Matt. 12:18-21).
He is King of kings and Lord of lords (Rev. 19:11-16).
He is the Sacrificial Lamb (Isa. 53:4-7).
He is Our Life (Col. 3:1-4).
He is the Light of the World (John 8:12).
He is Love (Rom. 5:8).

He is the One and Only (John 1:4).
He is our Peace (Eph. 2:14-18).
He is the Resurrection (John 11:25-26).
He is our Righteousness (Jer. 23:5-6).
He is Savior of the World (Luke 2:11-14).
He is the Son of God (Matt. 17:5).
He is the Bright Morning Star (Rev. 22:12-16).
He is the Way, the Truth, and the Life (John 14:6).

I challenge you, or as my kids say, "I double-dog-dare-you", at the beginning of each new day to read through and reflect on each of these Scriptures. In only a few minutes God can change your life through the truth of His Word.

I would like to emphasize the word *daily* because the world is geared toward convincing us that God is not Who He says He is. Satan's number-one priority and purpose for living is to distort God's truth. **One of the greatest tragedies—if not the greatest tragedy—with Americanized Christianity is that we have such a distorted view of God and His truth. This is the main reason we always can justify actions and attitudes that break His heart**.

The first and most important step to breaking free from all the play and pretending is to see God for who He really is. Such was the case with me. When I was broken—at the very bottom—in one of the poorest countries in all of Europe, I caught a glimpse of God. Catching a glimpse of God each day—learning more and more about Him each day—growing closer to Him each day will help more than anything else will in your personal battle with pretending and performing and with the shame that drives it.

When was the last time you spent time on your knees reflecting on Who God is? I guarantee that doing so will change your life. Remember that repentance begins with God and in seeing Him for Who He really is. When we repent, we refocus our attention on Him. **When we see Him for Who He really is, this enables us to take the next most important step for killing shame—exposing hypocrisy and breaking free from the prison of pretending.**

Expose "True Lies"

At one time we were foolish, disobedient, deceived and enslaved by all kinds of passions and pleasures. We lived in malice and envy, being hated and hating one another. But when the kindness and love of God our Savior appeared, he saved us, not because of righteous things we had done, but because of his mercy (Titus 3:3-5).

For it is by grace you have been saved, through faith—and this not from yourselves, it is the gift of God—not by works, so that no one can boast (Eph. 2:8-9).

Even though when I was younger, people made some accusations at me, those accusations weren't true. I'm no "girlie man." Speaking of Arnold Schwarzneggar, my favorite movie of his is *True Lies*. Talk about pretending! By day Arnold was a computer salesperson and by night a high-powered spy. He even fooled his wife and teen-aged daughter. As Arnold's disgruntled wife Jamie Lee Curtis was awesome in the show. Of course the truth of Arnold's secret life is revealed, the world is saved, and both husband and wife live happily ever after as they work as spies together. What Jamie Lee Curtis shared in a December 2004 interview with *Reader's Digest* was interesting. She stated, "Being an actor, you are recognized as being somebody else. Now all of a sudden I'm so less interested in pretending to be a lot of other people and much more interested in being me" (pp. 96-97). Maybe if Jamie Lee Curtis is less interested in pretending and being more real, maybe we as believers can do the same.

I do like the title of the movie, *True Lies*. Holding on to true lies is one of the main reasons we pretend. True lies are those things we believe as true even though they are false. For example we look at our past and think, "I'm a failure. I'm a loser. I've made so many mistakes. I'm no good. I don't deserve to be loved. I deserve to be punished." When we review our past, we also remember what our past critics said, "You're no good. You're a loser. You'll never amount to anything. Get lost." Tragically we begin to believe these lies as true. We certainly have plenty of evidence to support our conclusions. The important point to remember is this—what we believe to be true and what others believe to be true might not be true. Remember—at one time, everyone thought the world was flat. This is why basing our identity—who we believe we are in our hearts and minds—on truth, not on what we believe to be true is important. When we base our worth, our value, our identity on the truths found in God's Word, what we think about ourselves and what others think about us really doesn't matter. What matters most is what God thinks about us. God's truth is truth; it never will change.

As a professional counselor I firmly believe that our society's obsession with issues such as self-esteem, self-worth, and self-identity all are highly overrated. Self-esteem is made up of what we think about ourselves and what others think about us. The problem is that neither may be true. The problem is that each concept has self at the center. When we see God for Who He really is and see ourselves for Who we are in Him, we will have exactly the identity God desires us to have—a Christ-centered identity. A Christ-centered identity is the key to freedom from the prison of pretending.

Striving to be the best you can be won't set you free. Counseling won't set you free. Trying more diligently won't set you free. Only the truth will set you free. As Christians one of our huge problems is using constant self-improvement to feel better about ourselves. Keeping our self-esteem, self-worth, and self-confidence "pumped up" (as Arnold would say) always results in frustration and disappointment. This futile endeavor always perpetuates shame and our drive to perform.

Take an opportunity to catch a glimpse of who you are in Christ. I challenge you for the next 31 days to reflect on the following set of Scriptures each day. What is most important is not what you believe about yourself or what others believe about you but what God believes about you. Reflect on these truths that God desires for you to embrace in the deepest part of your heart and soul:

- I am alive (1 Cor. 15:22).
- I never am alone (Matt. 28:20).
- I belong (Eph. 2:19-20).

- I am capable (Phil. 4:13).
- I am forgiven (1 John 1:9).
- I am free (Rom. 3:24).
- I am God's friend (John 15:15).
- I am filled with joy (1 John 1:3-4).
- I am loved (Rom. 8:38).
- I am new (Eph. 4:22-24).
- I am powerful (2 Tim. 1:7).
- I am praised (Heb. 2:11-13).
- I am rich (Rom. 8:17).
- I am saved (Eph. 2:8, Rom. 10:9-10).
- I am secure (Col. 3:3-4).
- I am valuable (Matt. 5:13, Mark 9:50).
- I am wise (1 Cor. 1:30, James 1:5).
- I am without condemnation (Rom. 8:1).
- I have overcome; I'm a winner (Rev. 21:1-4).

You may have difficulty accepting these truths. These truths may be contrary to what you have been telling yourself or what others have been telling you for years—maybe even during your entire life. You may think, "That may be true for other Christians but not for me."

Another great tragedy among Christians is that we base our identity on what we believe about ourselves and on what others believe about us. In other words we trade the truth for what might or might not be true. When we create our own image, we can pretend to be whoever we want to be. The second most important step in breaking free from all the performing and pretending is seeing ourselves for who we really are in Christ.

Give yourself some time. Allow the truths of who you are in Christ, over time, to find their place in your heart and mind. Look up each of the Scriptures for yourself. Begin each day by opening your heart to Who God is and Who you are in Christ. I guarantee that your life will be radically transformed. A correct view of God and a correct view of who you are in Christ are absolutely necessary in breaking free from shame and the lies that perpetuate it.

Here is an important point. Don't miss this! When we see God for Who He really is and see ourselves for who we really are in Christ, we then can relate to others in ways that honor Him. As a result we discover open, honest, and real relationships with Christ and others. The show ends.

On a Personal Note . . .

Nothing helped me more in my own personal struggle with pretending and performing than to see God for Who he really is and to see myself or who I really am in Him. I believe these are the two most important and necessary keys to destroying shame at the roots and ending the show. Give it a try. You will not be disappointed. But it doesn't stop there. In the next section, look at a third recommendation for discovering a more real and authentic relationship with Christ.

Takin' It to the Streets

Remain in me, and I will remain in you. No branch can bear fruit by itself; it must remain in the vine. Neither can you bear fruit unless you remain in me. I am the vine; you are the branches. If a man remains in me and I in him, he will bear much fruit; apart from me you can do nothing (John 15:4-5).

The Lord replied, "My Presence will go with you, and I will give you rest" (Ex. 33:14).

Worship is not an event. Worship is the very reason for your existence. In other words your "quiet time" with the Lord each day is not to be a "check-off" of your list of things to do. Your quiet time is the attitude you are to take with you throughout the rest of the day. We are addressing suggestions for getting more real in your relationship with Christ. The first suggestion was to step out of the spotlight and allow Christ to have center stage. A second recommendation was to see yourself for who you really are in Christ based on the truths found in His Word. A third key to experiencing a more authentic Christian life requires taking your quiet times to the streets.

Make-Believers have "quiet times." They pray. They read their Bibles. They study the Scriptures. They are as knowledgeable of the Scriptures as is any Pharisee or Sadducee. The difference is that Make-Believers do not surrender control of their lives to Christ each day. The difference is that Make-Believers are not filled with the Spirit, do not pray to be filled with the Spirit, do not walk in the Spirit, and do not depend on the Spirit each and every day. Instead Make-Believers are consumed with their endless lists of responsibilities. Being led by and being filled with the Spirit is not supposed to stop after our quiet times are over. Our worship of the Lord is not supposed to end after our quiet times with Him are over or whenever the church service ends. Facing our daily responsibilities is the time we need the Holy Spirit's power and guidance more than ever. In other words we take our quiet times to the streets.

I see at least four requirements for taking your quiet time to the streets. The first requirement centers on how you relate or interact with others throughout the day. Silently pray for each person the Lord brings into your life for the day. I'm not talking about stopping and praying aloud for every person you see. I'm talking about *silently* praying for each person with whom you interact throughout the day. Pray that you would be an example of Christ to that person. Pray that you would interact with and respond to that person in a way that would bring the greatest glory to God. Pray that God's best and God's purpose would be accomplished in that person's life. This includes praying for all of the jerks and jerkettes that hack you off during the day.

No matter how you are treated—good or bad—pray that you would respond in a way that brings glory to God. Others don't even have to know you are praying for them. Simply take a moment to pray in your heart for them. See if God doesn't make a difference in your relationships and interactions with others. You might try beginning with the members of your own family.

Taking your quiet time to the streets requires submitting your relationships and interactions with others to Christ as Lord throughout the day. Second, taking your quiet time to the street requires submitting your endless responsibilities to Christ as Lord throughout the day. Through silent prayer submit your responsibilities to the Lord each day. Whether your responsibilities throughout the day are big or small, prayerfully submit them to Christ. Usually we pray about the big, huge, important things of life. Rarely—except in the case of Brother Lawrence—do we submit the ordinary, mundane, menial tasks of life.

Brother Lawrence, an humble cook in a French monastery, captured the practice of taking his time with the Lord throughout the day not only in his life but also in his classic book, *The Practice of the Presence of God* (pp. 5-9). Brother Lawrence was able to turn even the most commonplace of menial tasks, such as preparing meals and washing dishes, into acts of praise and communion with God. According to Brother Lawrence, the key to our obedience to Christ is not in changing what we do but in changing our hearts toward what we do. He said that we should begin doing for God what we normally do for ourselves or others, whether it was eating, bathing, working, relaxing, or taking out the trash. In other words surrender the very smallest and most menial tasks to the Lord and surrender the huge and overwhelming responsibilities to Him, as well. And whatever you do, do it all for the glory of God. Trust me; I never have taken out the trash in the same way again. Taking your quiet time to the streets requires surrendering your relationships and your responsibilities to Christ as Lord throughout the day.

Third, taking your quiet time to the streets requires radical obedience. Resolve to obey immediately as the Spirit leads throughout the day, no matter what the cost. Even begin to see as divine appointments your interruptions or even the unexpected. Unfortunately most of us believe that our time and what we do with our time are ours to control. Nothing could be further from the truth. Scripture tells us that we are not our own. Scripture tells us that we have been bought with a price. Most of us fill our calendars and "to-do" lists to overflowing with activity after activity and leave absolutely no time for the unexpected. When we do encounter interruptions or the frustrations of life, we become unglued. We gripe, complain, curse, get angry, and/or disregard the person needing our time and attention. We hate interruptions because we see others and unexpected situations as getting in the way of what we need to accomplish and to get done.

When we returned from the mission field (more about that later), we moved to Dallas. I have not adjusted to Dallas traffic. Some drivers would love to run over me or to see me dead for getting in their way. Why? Because I drive the speed limit (or five miles over). Dallas drivers would rather fight, scream, yell at each another, and flip each other off than to respond in kindness and to let someone else get in front of them. I never see more hate and aggression than when I get out in traffic. If Jesus truly is the Lord of our lives, then He is to be Lord of our time, even when someone else gets in our way. Commit the unexpected to the Lord. Pray for godly wisdom to deal with interruptions, the unexpected, and delays as opportunities to bring glory to Him. Mature Christians realize that life is not simply about their needs, feelings, rights, or schedules—even when driving in traffic.

The final requirement for taking your quiet time to the streets is to remain in an ongoing attitude of repentance and surrender. None of us is perfect. Even when our hearts are in the right places, from time to time we will fail or blow it. Confessing our sins, failures, or mistakes to God as quickly as possible is important. Quickly making things right with anyone we have harmed as a result of our selfishness or carelessness is important. We may be tempted to regard it as no big deal or to expect others to just get over it. When we make a big mistake, we may be tempted to try more urgently to make up for our failures. These kinds of reactions are what made "make-believers" out of us to begin with. We can do nothing to make up for our mistakes, sins, and failures. The past is the past. We can, however, repent, confess our sin, and trust that Christ is able and willing, day by day, to cleanse us from all unrighteousness. We are works in progress. You know what? Being a work in progress is OK.

Taking our faith to the streets and beyond the four walls of the church is no easy task. In fact, doing this is impossible in our own strength. Depend on Christ and the power of the Holy Spirit, which leads us to the next recommendation for getting more real in your relationship with Christ.

Re-Fill 'Er Up

So I say, live by the Spirit, and you will not gratify the desires of the sinful nature. Since we live by the Spirit, let us keep in step with the Spirit (Gal. 5:16, 25).

They chose Stephen, a man full of faith and of the Holy Spirit (Acts 6:5).

Be filled with the Spirit (Eph. 5:18).

Repeat the following sentences after me, "OK, Lord, I give up. You take control." Now try repeating these, "Lord I surrender all of who I am to you—my heart, my time, my agenda, and my all. As I surrender myself to you, please fill me with Your Holy Spirit." What do you think? Do you feel a little lighter? Do you feel a little freer? I have lived countless days of my Christian life in the flesh—in my own strength. Countless days have been spent getting done what I needed to get done. Then arrived the day I realized a big, huge, missing piece of the puzzle—the filling and guiding of the Holy Spirit. **A day not lived in the Spirit is a day lived in the flesh. No more exhausted, miserable, and resentful people exist on earth than Christians striving to live out the Christian life in their own strength.**

Each day take an opportunity to "fill 'er up." I realize gas prices are outrageous. Filling up the tank these days costs a small fortune. This is especially costly in the eight-passenger gas-guzzler my family drives. We keep spare gas cans in the trunk to get us from gas station to gas station. Hopefully by the time you read this book, gas prices will have gone way down. Filling up with the Holy Spirit is much different. Filling up with the Holy Spirit is free for the asking. Each day take an opportunity to pray and commit to God all of who you are. This kind of daily surrender is so crucial and so meaningful. Surrender to Him your relationships, your agenda, your time, your responsibilities, your life, and your all for the day. As you empty yourself before Him, pray for the Lord to fill you with His love and His Spirit. Pray for the filling of His Spirit to overflowing.

I happen to be a Baptist. Baptists are deathly afraid of the Holy Spirit. We don't want others to think that we have gone "Pentecostal"—jumping pews, and such. I believe that we are responsible for emptying ourselves so that He, the Holy Spirit, can fill our lives each day. When we are saved, the Holy Spirit lives in our hearts. He begins to dwell in us. That is God's promise. Our daily responsibility is to empty ourselves and allow Him, the Spirit, to fill us. We cannot possibly live a life of obedience without the daily filling and empowering of the Holy Spirit. Our lives may be filled with good deeds and religious activities. Our lives may be filled with striving to do what is right and avoiding what is wrong. We may be great ministers or writers or speakers or spouses or parents or employers or church members, but the truth remains—we can't live out the Christian life in our own strength. We can't earn the favor of God in our own strength. Pride would love to convince us that we can, but once again, the truth remains—a**s long as we are full of ourselves, we can't be filled with Him**.

Consider this following prayer—a prayer of surrender, emptying, and filling:

Heavenly Father, I know that I can't live the Christian life without you. Today, on my knees, I surrender to You all of who I am. I surrender my time, my agenda, my emotions, my will, my strength, my mind, my heart, my all to You as Lord. By Your Grace, may Your will be accomplished in my life for Your glory. Father, as I empty myself before You, I pray that You will fill me to overflowing with your Spirit. Shine Your love, Your mercy, and Your forgiveness through me. I pray that others would not see me or even my best. I pray that others would see You living through me, this day. Fill me to overflowing, I pray. In the Name of Jesus. Amen.

On a Personal Note . . .

I believe pride strives to convince us that we do not need Christ and the empowering of His Holy Spirit to live out the Christian life. Daily, ongoing, heartfelt, and humble prayers of surrender remind us that we do.

We simply do not take the time to soak in the best God has to offer. We do not take the time to re-fill, renew, or relax. We think by watching two or three hours of television a day that we are relaxing. Actually the opposite is true. Television drains us and robs us of the possibility of soaking in the good things of God. Our busy, overly stressed lives steal us from the very things we need to re-energize and to live abundant lives. These things include:

- quiet time with God
- time in His Word
- prayer for ourselves and others
- listening to great music
- hanging out with good friends
- sit-down meals with our families
- family devotionals
- watching a beautiful sunset
- going for a walk
- staring at the stars at night
- regular exercise
- eating right and healthy

- sharing our faith
- spending time with the elderly, widows, or orphans
- having a barbecue with the neighbors

We are no good for ourselves, for others, and for God because we always are running on empty. Fill up your heart and life with the Holy Spirit, feed your soul with the good things of God, focus on physical fitness through self-discipline in order to be your very best for God and the ones He has called you to love and serve.

Escape the Madness

Come to me, all you who are weary and burdened, and I will give you rest. Take my yoke upon you and learn from me, for I am gentle and humble in heart, and you will find rest for your souls. For my yoke is easy and my burden is light (Matt. 11:28-30).

We are driven to perform. We are driven to hide and to pretend. We are driven to excel, achieve, and accomplish. We are busier than ever and more exhausted than ever. The deeper our wounds from the past, the faster we go. Making up for yesterday always robs us of what is most important today.

As a result we may be "successful" on the outside, but inside we are miserable, angry, discouraged, and discontented. I don't think this is what Jesus meant when he said, "I have come that they may have life, and have it to the full" (John 10:10). We are full all right—full of ourselves. We can't slow down. We are on the go 24/7 and never take the time to disconnect from life's demands. We refuse to take the time to listen to the One with all the answers for our crazy and chaotic lives. And no, I'm not talking about listening to Oprah and to Dr. Phil.

Such was the case with a prominent but exhausted pastor serving in our city. He was so tired and exhausted, he finally agreed to go with his wife to the doctor's office. After his checkup the doctor called the wife alone into his office. He told the wife, "Your husband is suffering from horrible stress combined with severe exhaustion. He is completely and totally burned out. He simply is way too busy. If you don't do the following, your husband surely will die." The doctor then gave the wife his prescription. He said, "Each morning fix him a healthy breakfast. Be pleasant. Make sure he is in a good mood. For lunch make him a nutritious meal. For dinner prepare an especially nice meal. Don't burden him with chores. Don't discuss your problems with him; this only will make his stress worse. And most importantly, show him attention and affection and satisfy his every whim. If you can do this for the next 10 months to a year, I think your husband will live." On the way home the husband wondered why his wife spoke to the doctor for so long. Finally he asked his wife, "Well, what did the doctor say?" She replied, "You're gonna die."

Patrick Means stated the following about our out-of-control lifestyle: "The 90s-style, nonstop life has at least three lethal results: greater stress, less time for reflection, and an increased tendency to control those around us in the name of getting more things done. Under these conditions the first victims to fall usually are our healthiest habits: nurturing important relationships and taking time to deal with our own spiritual needs. Eventually the open-throttle lifestyle itself becomes a drug even as it burns out our bodies and minds and imperfectly masks our pain" (*Men's Secret Wars*, p. 173).

Quieting ourselves before the Lord requires the discipline to unplug from the demands of life. I hear you asking, "Quiet, what's that?" Peace and quiet requires the discipline to listen. A time to sit and be quiet and be still and listen to the Lord in that still, small, quiet voice will transform your relationship with Him. In fact having a deep and meaningful relationship with Christ without a time each day to spend with Him is impossible. Unplug the computer, the phone, and the television. Bury the cell phone in the back yard; take an opportunity to sit at the Master's feet. In the midst of your hurried life, make time simply to sit and listen. Sitting at the Master's feet is the only time we can be reminded of an absolutely crucial message: We are not valuable to God because of what we do; we are valuable to God because of who we are. We are His children.

Capture as many moments as you can today with Christ. Capture as many moments and make as many memories as you can with those you love. Time passes so quickly, so make the most of each moment. Don't wait for tragedy to remind you of what is most important in life. Erma Bombeck, in her column entitled "If I Had to Live My Life Over Again", writes: "I would have invited friends over to dinner even if the carpet was stained and the sofa faded. I would have sat on the lawn with my children and not worried about grass stains. I would never have bought anything just because it was practical, wouldn't show soil, or was guaranteed to last a lifetime. When my child kissed me impetuously, I would never have said, 'Later. Now get washed up for dinner.' There would have been more I love you's, more I'm sorry's, but mostly, given another shot at life, I would seize every minute, look at it and really see it, live it, and never give it back" (*Ragamuffin Gospel*, pp. 97-98).

Escape the madness, slow down, grab every moment, embrace it, and live it to the fullest.

Accent Accountability

Therefore confess your sins to each other and pray for each other so that you may be healed (Jas. 5:16).

Greater love has no one than this, that he lay down his life for his friends (John 15:13).

In all of our striving, in all of our accomplishments, in all of our successes, in all of our importance, we lose our "first love." As a result we look good on the surface, but in the process, we lose close, honest, open fellowship with Christ and others. In essence we become the Church at Ephesus. Jesus states: "I know your deeds, your hard work, and your perseverance. I know that you cannot tolerate wicked men, that you have tested those who claim to be apostles but are not, and have found them false. You have persevered and have endured hardships for my name, and have not grown weary. Yet I hold this against you: You have forsaken your first love" (Rev. 2:2-4).

Rediscover your first love for Christ and refocus your attention on Him. Then consider another critical recommendation for a more real Christian life: depend on each other.

Christ did not make us to live the Christian life on our own. We need each other; we need to hold each other accountable. In my personal opinion **we cannot grow in our faith or grow in our relationship with Christ without growing in our relationships with each other.**

In other words accountability relationships are a must. By accountability relationships I'm not talking about buddies with whom you "hang out" or even with whom you pray on a regular basis. I'm talking about trusted Christian friends who care enough to lovingly confront you about your greatest struggles with sin. Remember: the thing we hide is what makes us unhealthy; our secrets keep us sick. Accountability forces us to emerge from hiding.

According to statistics, 95 percent of Christian leaders choose to hide. Fewer than five percent report to having accountability relationships. Many others, however, understand the necessity of accountability relationships. In his book *Cultivating a Life for God,* Neil Cole provides 11 lists of accountability questions later published in *ChurchSmart Resources* in 1999 on pages 125-131. One of the lists recorded in this article is from Chuck Swindoll, one of my favorite authors of all time. He serves as pastor at the Stonebriar Community Church in Frisco, just north of Dallas. He also believes we were not designed to live the Christian life on our own. Throughout his ministry he has had his most trusted friends and fellow pastors ask him the following questions:

1. Have you been with a woman anywhere this past week in a situation that might be seen as compromising?
2. Have any of your financial dealings lacked integrity?
3. Have you exposed yourself to any sexually explicit material?

4. Have you spent adequate time in Bible study and prayer?
5. Have you given priority time to your family?
6. Have you fulfilled the mandates of your calling?
7. Have you just lied to me?

These are some excellent questions. They are the exact questions I give to my accountability partners. For me accountability relationships are an absolute necessity. You may think, "I don't need anybody to keep me in line. I don't believe in airing dirty laundry." I advise you to get ready for a fall.

On the mission field one of my best friends was Ben Hanna. He and his wife lived and served in the war-torn nation of Serbia. I never will forget the day he asked me to hold him accountable in his relationship with his spouse. He said, "Steve, don't be easy on me. Ask me the tough questions. If I'm not honest, if I step across the line, inform my immediate supervisor. I want it to cost me something." He truly is amazing. In the following "DO OUR PART" acronym look at the areas in which Ben desired accountability

- **D**ate—I will court my wife, pursue her, and let her know she is the most important person in the world to me.
- **O**nly—I will have eyes only for her. I will keep my eyes and my heart focused on my wife.

- **O**bey—I will study and obey God's commands, no matter what the cost.
- **U**nity—I will work to strengthen and not let anything threaten the unity between my wife and me.
- **R**ead—We will read God's Word each day individually, together as a couple, and together as a family.

- **P**ray—I will pray daily with my wife and my kids and for my wife and kids.
- **A**sk—I will ask my wife daily, "How are you? How can I pray for you? Do we have anything between us that we need to address?"

- **R**emember—I will remember and realize that she never is my enemy. Either Satan, my lack of leadership, passivity, and/or lack of Christlikeness is a major contributor to our conflict.
- **T**ell her I love her. I will tell her I love her in a way that has meaning for her, such as daily couch time, weekly date nights, helping out with the kids, helping out around the house, and keeping the finances in order.

I remember how Ben ended our conversation that day in one of the most beautiful places on earth—Bled, Slovenia. He said, "It's time for us, as Christian men, to do our part." Amen to that, brother!

The time has arrived for each of us to do our part in confronting the sin in our lives. Jesus said, "If your right eye causes you to sin, gouge it out and throw it away. It is far better for you to lose one part of your body than for your whole body to be thrown into hell. And if your right hand causes you to sin, cut it off and throw it away. It is better for you to lose one part of your body than for your whole body to go into hell" (Matt. 5:29-30).

I don't think Jesus is encouraging us to start hacking off body parts. I do believe that He is calling us to be radical in confronting the sin in our lives—whatever is required. The first step is being honest about the sin in our lives. Scripture states, "If we claim to be without sin, we deceive ourselves and the truth is not in us" (1 John 1:8). If you don't think you have a serious sin problem in your life and that you don't need people who genuinely care to help you confront that sin, you only fool yourself.

Pray and ask God to bring to mind someone who might be a potential accountability partner. Make this someone of the same gender with whom you already have a close and trusting relationship. I always recommend testing the waters. Accountability relationships take time and require some risk. Hence, confidentiality and Christian maturity are crucial. Begin by sharing with your potential partner some personal prayer requests. Wait for a period of time to see if that information returns to bite you. If you and the information are respected, try sharing more personal information.

Eventually you might get to the point in which you feel comfortable asking the tough questions, "Will you be my accountability partner? And, will you ask me the following questions from time to time?" Getting to this point is not easy. It requires courage and vulnerability, but it is worth the risk.

If you can develop accountability relationships with two or three other Christians, then praise the Lord. Accountability partners are worth their weight in gold. Why have two or three accountability partners—not including your spouse? You easily can fool another person and manipulate your spouse with lines such as, "Everything is OK. I'll change. Quit griping at me. You're just as bad."

Much more difficult is fooling a few close and trusted friends of the same gender who have your best interests at heart. Scripture states, "Though one may be overpowered, two can defend themselves. A cord of three strands is not quickly broken" (Ecc. 4:12). Scripture also states, "Plans fail for lack of counsel, but with many advisors they succeed" (Prov. 15:22).

On a Personal Note . . .

Stepping out of the spotlight and allowing God to have center stage and seeing myself for who I really am in Christ were huge in ending the pretending and performance for me. Equally important and more than anything else, accountability relationships have kept me going in the right direction. If you desire a more real and genuine relationship with Christ, emerge from hiding and allow others to hold you accountable.

Love More and Expect Less

Jesus replied, "'Love the Lord your God with all your heart and with all your soul and with all your mind.'" This is the first and greatest commandment. And the second is like it: 'Love your neighbor as yourself.' All the Law and the Prophets hang on these two commandments" (Matt. 22:37-40).

After we completed our first term of service in Moldova, we returned to the United States for our first Stateside Assignment. Near the end of our six-month stay we prepared to return to Moldova with our nearly 4-year-old daughter, Sarah; 2-year-old daughter, Abigail; and our 6-month-old son, Joshua Steven, when I received an important phone call. Our new regional leader for Central and Eastern Europe (CEE), Rodney Hammer, was in the U.S. and asked me to visit with him. At that meeting he asked me to move my family from Moldova to Prague, Czech Republic, to become the member-care consultant for the CEE region. Karen and I prayed about this request and felt God leading us to make this move. We returned to Moldova for a few months, tied up loose ends, and said goodbye to all our friends and colleagues. We moved to Prague in September 2000. As I began my new position, we started studying the Czech language part-time.

In May 2002 the Lord added a fourth child to our family. Anna Joy was born in Prague. I enjoyed my work ministering to the missionaries in the areas of pastoral care, Missionary Kid education, and medical needs.

I became such a "people pleaser"—striving to surpass everyone's expectations—especially my own. I was traveling out of the country 60 percent of the time. I always had a suitcase packed and ready for my next trip. I basically left my wife alone to rear our four kids—all ages 6 and under—in Prague, Czech Republic. My fellow missionaries called my wife a "missionary widow." I craved the attention and applause from the conferences, dinners, and ministry in 25 countries spanning 12 time zones across Central and Eastern Europe. The more I traveled, the more exhausted I became and the more I missed my family.

So, there I was in the beautiful city of Vilnius, the capital of Lithuania, in North Central Europe. I spent the morning providing "top-quality pastoral care" to a missionary family literally falling apart at the seams. Here was a family that sacrificed everything to share God's love with others in a faraway land. At the same time they had no time, no energy, and no desire to share love with each other. At first this situation made no sense. How could working for God kill your family life? Does God really desire for us to neglect our families and our closest relationships for Him.

During the next four days these family members and I examined how missions was killing what was most important in life—their love for Christ and their love for each other. I learned a lesson I never will forget. **The great things we do for God can rob us of our love for Him and our love for each other.**

Each evening, with these insights heavy on my mind and heart, I left this dear family and walked to my hotel. I enjoyed the evening breeze and walking through the winding Vilnius streets, as I passed by the capitol building, cut through the downtown square, and stopped by a nearby market to buy my favorite candy bar on the way to my hotel room. My room was so quiet without kids yelling, screaming, crying, vomiting, pooping, fussing, fighting, griping, and complaining. I turned on some Lithuanian television to attempt to drown out the silence. Unfortunately I couldn't understand *Everybody Loves Raymond* or *CSI: Miami* in Lithuanian. So I began to read a book that I was planning to give away as a gift. It was going to make the perfect parting gift for this struggling missionary family. I never thought that my "going-away gift" was the exact book that God intended as a "going-away gift" for me.

The powerful little book I read was entitled *Choosing to Cheat* by Andy Stanley. It's my kind of book—short, small, and to the point. The quote that so captured my attention was the following:

> Reprioritizing your world around your family is not just a good idea. It is a God idea. As a Christian, I don't think I have any option when it comes to establishing my priorities. To ask my family to take the leftovers is more than insensitive. It flies in the face of everything we are taught in the New Testament about the family (p. 74.)

Those words pierced my soul. I began to feel sick at my stomach. Maybe it was the candy bar. Stanley went on to state:

> Everybody cheats. Don't cheat the people who love you most. Don't cheat the person who is looking forward to spending the rest of his or her life with you. Don't cheat yourself of the peace that comes with knowing that you are squarely in the will of the One who created you. Don't cheat your kids of the security that comes with knowing they are Mommy and Daddy's priority (p. 110).

The truth was that **my family was in a state of emergency. I was cheating my wife and family. My mistress was the most beautiful, deadly, and seductive of all mistresses. My mistress was not flesh and bone. My mistress was ministry.** My mistress was success. My mistress was significance. My heart didn't belong to the Lord, my spouse, or my kids. My heart belonged to my mistress.

I always had bragged about being a "family man." The truth was that I dedicated my life to meeting the needs of others while I expected my family to meet mine. I expected my wife to meet my needs. I expected my wife to serve me. I expected my kids to mind me and to do what I say. I know you are going to think I'm crazy and definitely slow. After nearly 13 years of marriage and six kids, I realized that my wife and my kids were not put on this earth to serve me. Those closest to me were put on this earth to give me the opportunity to demonstrate Christ's love. I firmly believe in the saying, "Who you really are is who you are at home." **Treat the members of your family better than you do anyone else on earth; you will solve at least 90 percent of your problems at home.**

My brother-in-law is in law school, so he hears the best and worst stories about the legal profession. I really enjoyed one story about a high-powered, Houston lawyer who counseled a Christian man who wanted to divorce his wife. He told the lawyer he wanted to really teach her a lesson. He said he wanted to really "do her dirty." The lawyer said, "Listen. I'll tell you what to do. I have the perfect plan. For the next three months, treat your wife like a queen.

Love her, meet her every need, cherish her, clean up around the house, and take care of the kids. Then, after three months, serve her the paper and drop her like a red-hot potato." An odd thing happened. When the husband began to love and serve his wife, she was transformed. She became exactly the woman he always desired. He was transformed. She was transformed. The marriage was transformed. To this day they are married.

The truth is—if we treated our fellow church members as we treated the members of our own family, we would be excommunicated. If we treated our co-workers as we treated the members of our own family, we would be fired on the spot. If we treated any boss as we treat our own spouses, we never would be employed again. **I believe that most of us spend the majority of our lives trying to get our family members to do what we want them to do and to be who we want them to be. Tragically this leaves little, if any, opportunity for God to do what He wants to do in us.**

If you don't remember anything else in this book, remember this: if we were to treat the members of our family as well as we treat those we desperately strive to please, we instantly would see life-changing results in our homes—guaranteed! I left the mission field and my prestigious, international ministry so I could discover what real love and service was all about, beginning in my own home.

In April 2003 I interviewed for and accepted my current job as professor at The Criswell College. I bought a house without Karen even seeing it. (This was an accomplishment, since underwear and socks usually are difficult decisions for me.) After the Dallas interview I returned to Prague, Czech Rpublic to say goodbye to our missionary and national friends. We were heartbroken to leave them; we still miss the field—terribly.

In the midst of another move, tragedy struck when, in June 2003, Karen miscarried a child. Excitement was mixed with grief as we began our new life in the States in July 2003.

My last recommendation for you to experience a more real Christian life is to love the members of your family. Love them, serve them, forgive them, and accept them no matter what the cost. Watch the transformation begin.

Freedom!

The moment you stop expecting others to love you, approve of you, applaud you, or even appreciate you is the day you will discover freedom. When you let go of proving, performing, and expecting, you can become the person God intends you to be. You can't possibly be disappointed when you don't have the expectations of others. When you live for God, He never disappoints. When you live for God, you discover the best part of who you are. **The best part of who you are is who you are in Christ on the inside, not who you pretend to be on the outside.**

Can you hear him? I can hear Mel Gibson stretched out and yelling, "Freedom!" Hey, he's not the only Braveheart. When you let go of the expectations, the striving, and the proving, you become "bravehearted" as well. Christ-centered confidence is born the moment you let go of expectations, live to please Christ, and trust the results to Him.

Remembering Jenny

I drive my kids to school every day. We were listening to the radio when we heard a story about a 7-year-old girl named Jenny. Jenny spotted a pearl necklace in a dime store and just had to have those fake pearls. She worked every day. She cleaned the garage, set up a lemonade stand, cleaned her room, helped around the house, and promptly put her earnings in her piggy bank. Her grandma surprised her with a new crisp, dollar bill.

Jenny finally had the money she needed to buy the necklace. It became her most prized possession. She wore the necklace all the time. Her parents were so proud of her and loved her so much. One evening as her dad put her to bed, he asked his daughter, "Jenny, how about giving me your pearl necklace?" Jenny objected, "No, Daddy, please. I'll give you my favorite doll. You can take any of my toys. Please don't take my necklace." "It's OK, honey. Don't worry," her dad replied as he gently kissed her on the cheek. A few days later her dad once again asked his daughter for the pearls. "Please, Daddy. Anything but my pearls," she cried. "I worked so hard to get them." He said, "It's OK, honey. Don't worry," and gave her a gentle kiss on the cheek as he left the room.

The next night when the time arrived for evening Bible study and prayer, Jenny sat on the corner of her bed and clasped her pearls. With a quivering lip and a tear rolling down her cheek, she gave to her father her most prized possession. No sooner had she given away her necklace than her father pulled from his pocket a case with a string of genuine pearls for his child. All Jenny had to do was to let go of her dime-store imitation to get the real thing.

The same is true in our relationship with Christ. The Lord desires for us to let go of our most prized possessions—even those we work so diligently to earn. **No sooner do we turn over our dime-store, imitation faith than He replaces it with the real thing.**

Arise and Walk

Dr. Lamar Cooper and his wife, Barbara, are two of the finest Christians I know. Dr. Cooper serves as the vice-president of academic affairs at The Criswell College where I teach. At age 8 his grandson, Jonathan Cooper, suffered a diabetic coma. One minute he was a beautiful, fun-loving, young boy; the next, he was lying lifeless in the hospital and depending on machines to keep him alive. The doctors told his parents to "Pull the plug. We can do nothing for him." Another doctor stated, "If anything happens, God will have to do it. The boy is beyond hope." Family members said their goodbyes, joined in prayer with literally thousands of Christians around the world, and disconnected Jonathan from the machines. Since that day the family has seen Jonathan begin to breathe on his own. After a tremendous and tough battle, the family and doctors have seen Jonathan not only emerge from the coma but also feed himself, talk, and even tell jokes. In chapel at The Criswell College, while failing to hold back my tears, I shook

Jonathan's hand and hugged his grandparents. Jonathan told us all, "Thanks for praying for me. God has worked miracles, but I still have a long way to go." Jonathan taught me an important lesson. **When we unplug from all the things that we think keep us alive, God is able to work real miracles.**

Let Go

Be kind and compassionate to one another, just as in Christ God forgave you (Eph. 4:32).

I know. I added an extra "L" to the acrostic, but we can't move forward until we address this last key. The last key in moving toward a more real relationship with Christ is to let go. Let go of the unresolved hurt and anger from your past. Resentment, or the unwillingness to forgive, always leads you and those closest to you down the road to destruction. **The unwillingness to forgive is at the heart of the majority of our spiritual, emotional, mental, relational—even physical problems of life.**

In her local Texas community Sally Johnson ministers to AIDS patients. Through personal visits, phone calls, emails, buying groceries, and providing support and encouragement, she demonstrates God's love to those "outcasts." The most difficult challenge by far, she says, is embracing her friends in their last few moments of life. Sally's greatest prayer is to be loved in the same way when her time arrives. Sally has AIDS as well. She contracted the disease 17 years ago when she was gang-raped by three men. Not only did she forgive the men who raped her and set in motion her death, she visited them in prison, served them, befriended them, and ultimately held each of them, one by one, as they lost the battle to the ravaging consequences of AIDS.

As she ended her presentation at The Criswell College in Dallas, she said: "For 17 years I have been living with AIDS. I believe God has kept me alive so long for two reasons. The first reason is because I forgave the guys that signed my death sentence so many years ago. And second, obviously, God has many more people to love through me."

It truly was one of the most powerful testimonies I ever had heard. Sally takes away every excuse I have not to forgive. Let go of your excuses. Let go of your pride, forgive, and discover more real and deeper relationships with Christ and others.

You're in the Spotlight

Take an opportunity to place God in the spotlight. Focus your attention on Him. take an opportunity to focus on who He is, who you are in Christ, and His great love for you as you reflect on the following questions:

1. As you read through the Scripture describing who Christ is and who you are in Christ, what were your reactions, your thoughts, and feelings?

2. My colleagues in the counseling and psychology fields think I'm crazy because I believe working to build a person's self-esteem, self-confidence, and self-identity are a waste of time. I tell them I don't like the focus on the word *self.* I tell them that as Christians, what we think or feel about ourselves or what others might say doesn't really matter. I tell them when we see God for who He really is and see ourselves for who we really are in Christ, the result always is experiencing true value, true worth, and Christ-centered identity. Would you argue for or against me, and why?

3. Do you really believe that you can do nothing to increase or decrease God's love for you? Do you truly believe that He loves you with every ounce of His love at this very moment from now throughout the rest of eternity? Explain your answer.

4. Would you describe your "quiet times" as a check-off on your list of things to do? Why or why not?

5. One of the huge missing elements in my Christian life was being filled and led by the Holy Spirit day by day, step by step. Describe the role of the Holy Spirit in your life.

6. Before you move to the next section, put away this book and all of your materials. Go for a nice walk in a pretty place. Thank the Lord for His unlimited blessings and undying love. Consider and pray about the practical steps you need to take to "get more real" in your relationship with Christ.

Stepping into God's Light

Heavenly Father,

We pray for a fresh understanding of who You are. Heavenly Father, we pray by your grace and mercy to see You face to face. Thank You for reminding us that only when we see You for who You really are that we are able to see ourselves for who we really are, in You. As a result, we will relate to You and to others in a way that brings honor to You. In other words, the show—the pretending—ends. Lord, thank You for reminding us of the absolute necessity of the Holy Spirit in living out the Christian life. We cannot live the Christian life in our own strength! We need You and we need each other to take our faith to the streets. Whether they realize it or not, people in a lost and dying world are crying out for Christians, who are real, to point them to You. Heavenly Father, thank You for these crucial reminders.

Now, heavenly Father, we praise You for your presence as we move into this final chapter describing the results of getting more real with You. End the pretending, Lord. Transform us.

We pray in the Name of Jesus. Amen.

Chapter 11

Living Happily Ever After

I have come that they may have life, and have it to the full (John 10:10).

For 17 years as a Christian I lived a lie. I lived in a dream world. I simply was "make-believing." As a Christian I thought success, popularity, belonging, praise, approval, and even significance were what I needed most in life. I wanted to be "happy." I thought I could find happiness outside of Christ. What I discovered was a lesson I'll never forget. The most miserable people on earth are Christians trying to find happiness through what the world has to offer. I discovered what I needed the most was an open, honest, genuine, daily walk and fellowship with the resurrected Christ. This is the purpose for which we were made. Nothing else will satisfy. This is what "living happily ever after" is all about. True contentment, true satisfaction, and real happiness are found only in the Person of Jesus Christ—and in Him alone.

The changes I experienced in my own life as a result of working through and recording this material were nothing short of miraculous. I experienced an amazing transformation unlike that of any other time in my life outside of trusting Christ as Savior 20 years ago.

I know what you're thinking: "Duh! Of course when you daily surrender your life to Christ, depend on Him, and are filled and led by the Holy Spirit, you will see some amazing changes." I just wish sometimes I wasn't such a slow learner. Let's close our time together by looking at some of the miraculous changes that are in store for you as you seek a more real and authentic relationship with Christ. Among the biggest changes you will experience will be in how you see God, in how you see yourself, in how you see others, and one of the greatest changes of all—in learning that performance ends. One by one let's examine these changes more closely.

In How You See God

Make-believers view God more like they do a parent than they do anything else. He is the One who is supposed to be there for them. He is to serve, help, guide, do this, and do that for them. He is to bail them out of this problem or that problem. He is supposed to work everything out for them. In return they will be "good Christians" or "good children." They actually seem to believe they can manipulate God into giving them what they want based on their good behavior. What's more, because of their good behavior, they believe they deserve the best things of God. When they don't get what they want, or when things don't work out as they want, they blame and re-take control. They get mad, pout, turn their backs on God, and take what they want. I know. It sounds completely and totally immature.

Real believers are much different. Real believers love God and serve Him even when life, circumstances, or relationships do not work out as they want. Real believers focus more on their responsibility to God and less on His responsibility to them. For real believers Jesus is Lord no matter what the cost, no matter what the circumstances, and no matter what the results. Real believers serve the Lord and others, not just when doing so is to their advantage or in their best interest. When you follow the recommendations in this book, when you step out of the spotlight and allow God to have center stage, when you see yourself for who you really are in Christ, when you take your faith to the streets in the power of the Holy Spirit, when you love more and expect less, beginning in your own home, your view of God will change. One reader shared that as a result of working through this material, not only was his view of God transformed, his prayers were transformed as well. I was honored when he permitted me to record one of his prayers here:

Heavenly Father, You are God; I am not. You are the Alpha and Omega. You are the Lord of lords and King of kings. You are God of all. You're the all-knowing, all-powerful, all-loving, and Almighty God. I can do no good thing to increase Your love for me. I can do no bad thing to diminish Your love for me. As I pray and reflect on the amazing nature of Your love, I pray for the grace to return that love to You today. I pray today for the grace and power to live a life that both publicly and privately brings glory and honor to Your Name. I pray for the grace to share Your love with others. Others do not need to see me. They need to see You. I pray that others would not see my best. I pray that others would see You. Heavenly Father, I pray for the grace to love You, serve You, and obey You as Lord no matter what the cost, no matter what the circumstances, no matter what the results. I pray these things in the precious Name of Your Son, Jesus. Amen.

In How You See Yourself

You will have major changes in how you see God and in how you relate to God. You also will have major changes in how you see yourself. Make-believers are plagued by self-destructive messages. They listen to these lies so much that they begin to believe them in their hearts. Make-believers believe they are no good. They believe they deserve to be punished. They are insecure and fearful. Accomplishments, achievements, and applause never are good enough to drown out the hurt of these lies.

Real believers are much different. Real believers allow the truths of God's Word to transform their hearts and minds. They know they are people of true value and true worth. They are not prisoners of their own unreasonable expectations and of the endless expectations of others. They are free. One reader shared how thankful she was to be free from the lies that plagued her throughout the course of her entire Christian life. She said she was so moved by the prayers this book records that she began to write out some of her own prayers. She gave me permission to share with you the following prayer:

> Heavenly Father, I feel so free. Thank You for reminding me that my value is not based on my performance. My value is not based on whether I do all of the things I am supposed to do. Thank You for reminding me that Your love is not based on whether I succeed or fail. This is so freeing for me. Your love is not based on whether I meet my own expectations or the expectations of others. Heavenly Father, thank You for the truth that Your love never changes. Your love for me never will change. Your love for me is based on Who You are and not on what I do. You love me. You always will love me. I am your child. And nothing ever will change that.. God, thank You for loving me and for forgiving me every day. Lord, thank You for never turning Your back on me and never giving up on me. I love you. I pray in Your Precious Name. Amen.

In How You See Others

Besides how you see God and how you view yourself, another big change will be in how you relate to and see others. Make-believers see God's main function as meeting their personal needs. No wonder they see others in much the same way! They believe others are placed on earth to meet their needs and to make them happy, as well. Their Christian lives are self-centered, self-glorifying lives.

On the other hand real believers are much different. Real believers see others as opportunities to demonstrate God's love. Their love freely and generously is given with no strings attached. Each day their prayer is to surrender their lives, dreams, ambitions, desires, needs, will, strength, and their all to Christ to glorify Him—beginning in their own homes. After reading the book one reader shared about her continued fear of others. She said the following daily prayer really has helped her in this ongoing challenge:

> Heavenly Father, You know my heart. I am afraid of others. I'm afraid of getting hurt or rejected or criticized. Or, I wait and let others make the first move. I expect them to take the initiative to be nice to me, serve me, meet my needs, and make me happy. Most of the time I'm simply too tired to care about others or too wrapped up in my own agenda or worries to care about anybody else. Heavenly Father, forgive me for my selfishness, my laziness, my lack of concern, my inability to love. Today, I pray, by Your grace, for the ability to share Your love. Father, channel Your love, Your mercy, Your forgiveness, Your heart to serve through me for the glory of Your Name and the furthering of Your Kingdom. I pray in the Name of Jesus. Amen.

In How Your See Your Circumstances

As you begin to break free from hiding and pretending, you also will see your circumstances differently. First of all, God uses the difficult circumstances of people and life to grow us, build our character, and prepare us for the purpose He desires us to fulfill. The tough times will make us bitter or better, depending on whether we trust in Him or trust in ourselves.

I love watching movies. All of my favorite movies have a similar theme—the main character overcomes great odds to accomplish great things. This same story appears in *Gladiator, Braveheart, Spartacus, Rudy, Star Wars,* and *Finding Nemo*. It gets me every time. God uses the tough times of life to prepare us to bring glory to Him. I never thought I would say this, but I am thankful for the devastating times in my past, because I am thankful for the person God has made me to be and for the person He continues to make me to be.

Secondly, you will discover that faith is not the absence of fear or doubt. Faith is taking the next obedient step when everything within you says, "Hide!", and everyone around you says, "Be quiet!" The victory always is in taking the next step of obedience, not in whether you succeed or fail. But remember this: a third lesson you will learn as you become more free in being the person God intends for you to be is that you always will have critics. Criticism that always hurts the most is from family members and fellow Christians. Since I began working on this material and circulated my manuscript, friends and peers have criticized and questioned me:

Are you emotionally disturbed?
Are you crazy?
Are you a sissy?
Are you fragile?
Do I know you?
What's wrong with you?

Then why publish the material? **The possibility of helping one person always makes the risk worthwhile.**

Regarding the circumstances of life, I have a favorite, personal prayer:

> Dear Lord, don't let success go to my head or failure to my heart. Lord, please help me remember that failure is an event—not a person. Just because I fail does not mean that I'm a failure. Just because I am criticized and rejected doesn't mean that the other person is right and I am wrong. Help me always to remember that You value me and love me, whether I succeed or fail. I pray in the Name of Jesus. Amen.

In Moving from Performance to Obedience

For the eyes of the Lord range throughout the earth to strengthen those whose hearts are fully committed to him (2 Chron. 16:9).

You'll have changes in how you see God, in how you see yourself, in how you see others, and in how you see your circumstances. The last and most dramatic change you will experience as you become more real in your relationships with Christ and others is moving from performance to obedience. This is one of the most significant and freeing changes of all. One interesting thing is that both obedience and performance appear on the surface to be the same. The main difference is not on the surface. The main difference is in the heart. Look at some of the most important differences between performance and obedience:

- Performance is characterized by success, exhaustion, resentment, discouragement, and fear. Obedience is characterized by love, joy, peace, patience, kindness, gentleness, goodness, and self-control.
- Performance takes charge of meeting its own needs and desires. Obedience trusts in Christ no matter what the results.
- Performance pretends. Performance is holy in public and hateful at home. Obedience is integrity. Obedience brings honor to God, whether in public or private.
- Performance strives for success and lives to impress. Obedience lives to honor God.
- A life of pretending and performing guarantees that feelings of worthlessness, insecurity, and inferiority are passed on to others—especially those who are closest. A life of obedience guarantees that God's love, value, significance, and worth are passed on to others, beginning with those who are closest.

When the pretending ends, you will have a blockbuster season. You will be transformed in how you view God, in how you view yourself, in how you relate to others, and in how you see your circumstances as you live a life of obedience filled and empowered by the Holy Spirit. After striving in futility to earn love, approval, and acceptance, you will, once again, rediscover your first love for Christ and others and discover what living happily ever after truly means.

Your Last Time in the Spotlight

We have been on an incredible journey together. Thank you for the privilege of allowing me to walk with you and to share my story with you. For your last "in-the-spotlight" exercise, please email me and share how the Lord has used this material to shed light into areas of your own life. I am so thankful for those who already have shared their response to the book. I have so valued their input. My prayer for you is that God would richly bless you as you continue to grow in a deeper and more meaningful relationship with Him. I'd love to hear from you at: *shunter@criswell.edu*

A Final Word of Prayer

Heavenly Father,

Thank You once again for this incredible journey. In this closing time of prayer we ask that You might give us a fresh glimpse of Who You are. Enable us to see ourselves and others through Your eyes. Empower us to love others, forgive others, and serve others in Your strength. Lord Jesus, transform our pretending, performing, and pleasing into Christ-centered obedience for the glory of Your Name and the furthering of Your Kingdom as we end the pretending and begin real living.

We pray in the Name of Jesus. Amen.

About the Author

Dr. Steve T. Hunter was a youth minister and pastor for nine years in Texas before he moved overseas to serve for seven years as a missionary in Central and Eastern Europe. He teaches as professor of counseling and psychology at The Criswell College in Dallas, TX, and serves on staff as a Christian counselor at First Baptist Church of Dallas. He has undergraduate, master's, and doctoral degrees in counseling and psychology from Texas A&M University in College Station and Commerce, TX. He has a master of divinity degree from Southwestern Baptist Theological Seminary in Fort Worth, TX, and a second doctoral degree in pastoral ministries from Mid-America Baptist Theological Seminary in Germantown, TN. He and his wife are involved in what he calls "organized chaos" as they rear their six children (five girls and one boy) in Rowlett, TX.

The Hunter family, back row, from left: Karen holds Jordan, Steve holds Julia. Front row, from left: Sarah, Abby, Josh, and Anna Joy.

References and Recommended Reading

Adderholdt, Miriam. *Perfectionism: What's Bad About Being Too Good* (Minneapolis: Free Spirit, 1999).

Arteburn, Stephen. *More Jesus, Less Religion: Moving from Rules to Relationships* (Colorado Springs: Waterbrook Press, 2000).

Bolsinger, Tod. *Show Time: Living Down Hypocrisy by Living Out the Faith* (Grand Rapids: Baker Books, 2004).

Bombeck, Erma. "If I Had to Live My Life Over", *Saturday Evening Post*, 253, Nov. 1981, 17, and reprinted in the *Reader's Digest*, 120 April 1982, 150.

The Practice of the Presence of God: Conversations and Letters of Brother Lawrence (Lightheart Edition, *www.PracticeGods Presence.com).*

Cole, Neil. *Cultivating a Life for God* (St. Charles: IL: ChurchSmart Resources, 1999).

Fischer, John. *12 Steps for the Recovering Pharisee*. (Minneapolis: Bethany House Publishers, 2000).

Greenspon, Thomas. *Freeing Our Families from Perfectionism.* (Minneapolis: Free Spirit, 2002).

Hendricks, William. *Exit Interviews*. (Chicago: Moody, 1993).

Manning, Brennan. *The Ragamuffin Gospel*. (Sisters, OR: Multnomah, 2000).

Means, Marsha. *Living with Your Husband's Secret Wars* (Grand Rapids: Revell, 2002).

Means, Patrick. *Men's Secret Wars* (Grand Rapids: Revell, 1999).

Peters, Holly, "Evangelicals on the Decline," *The Biola Connection*, Fall, 2002.

Smith, Ann. *Overcoming Perfectionism: the Key to Balanced Recovery* (Deerfield Beach, FL: Health Communication, 1990).

Stanley, Andy. *Choosing to Cheat: Who Wins When Family and Work Collide* (Sisters, OR: Multnomah, 2003).

Stoop: David. *Hope for the Perfectionist* (Nashville: Thomas Nelson, 1989).

Warren, Rick. *The Purpose Driven Life* (Grand Rapids: Zondervan, 2002).

Order more copies of

Make-Believers

Call toll free: 1-800-747-0738

Visit: ***www.hannibalbooks.com***

Email: ***hannibalbooks@earthlink.net***

FAX: 1-888-252-3022

Mail copy of form below to:

Hannibal Books
P.O. Box 461592
Garland, Texas 75046

Number of copies desired ________________

Multiply number of copies by $12.95 ________________

Please add $3 for postage and handling for first book and add 50 cents for each additional book in the order.

Shipping and handling$____________

Texas residents add 8.25% sales tax $____________

Total order $___________

Mark method of payment:

check enclosed ________________________________

Credit card# __________________________________

exp. date____ (Visa, MasterCard, Discover, American Express accepted)

Name ______________________________________

Address ____________________________________

City State, Zip _______________________________

Phone ____________________ FAX _________________

Email ______________________________________

You'll enjoy these inspiring books also

Be a 24/7 Christian by Wade Akins. Want to make Jesus truly the Lord your life but don't know how? This renowned missionary evangelist/strategist tells how to live the adventure of being totally sold out to the Lord every moment of every day, every day of every year.

______Copies at $9 .95=________

Servant on the Edge of History by Sam James. What led American Sam James to allow himself and his family to be in harm's way again and again during war-traumatized Vietnam? Read this untold story of the Vietnam Era, when members of the James family constantly risked their lives for the gospel in order to help their beloved Vietnamese people.

______Copies at $9 .95=________

Way Back in the Country by Kay Moore. Join the antics of the Three Red-Haired Miller Girls as their farm family shares six generations of recipes and the stories behind them.

______Copies at $9 .95=________

When the Heart Soars Free by Kay Moore. A heart-touching love story with a healing, biblical message. Set in a picturesque mountain wonderland.

______Copies at $9 .95=________

Add $3.00 shipping for first book, plus 50 cents for each additional book.

Shipping & Handling ____________

Texas residents add 8.25% sales tax ________

TOTAL ENCLOSED____________

check ____ or credit card # __________________ exp. date_________

(Visa, MasterCard, Discover, American Express accepted)

Name ____

Address ____________________________ Phone ____________

City __________________ State ____________ Zip __________

For postal address, phone number, fax number, email address and other ways to order from Hannibal Books, see page 173.